100 DAYS OF
GRACE
for WOMEN

FAMILY

Christian Stores

Printed in the United States of America

100 DAYS OF
GRACE

for WOMEN

TABLE OF CONTENTS

INTRODUCTION

How desperately our world needs Christian women who are willing to honor God with their praise, their prayers, and their service. Hopefully, you are determined to become such a woman—a woman who walks in wisdom as she offers counsel and direction to her family, to her friends, and to her coworkers.

This generation faces problems that defy easy solutions, yet face them we must. We need women whose vision is clear and whose intentions are pure. And this book can help.

In your hands, you hold a book that contains 100 devotional readings that are intended to remind you of God's love and God's grace. During the next 100 days, please try this experiment: read a chapter each day. If you're already committed to a daily worship time, this book will enrich that experience. If you are not, the simple act of giving God a few minutes each morning will change the direction and the quality of your life.

As you consider your own circumstances, remember this: whatever the size of your challenge, whatever the scope of your problem, God is bigger. Much bigger. He will instruct you, protect you, energize you, and heal you if you let Him. So let Him. Pray fervently, listen carefully, work diligently, and treat every single day as an opportunity for praise and worship because that's precisely what every day can be . . . and should be.

THE GIFT OF GRACE, FREELY GIVEN

For all have sinned, and fall short of the glory of God,
being justified freely by His grace through
the redemption that is in Christ Jesus. . . .

Romans 3:23-24 NKJV

Romans 3:23 reminds us that all of us fall short of the glory of God. Yet despite our imperfections and despite our shortcomings, God sent His Son so that we might be redeemed from our sins. In doing so, our Heavenly Father demonstrated His infinite mercy and His infinite love.

We have received countless gifts from God, but none can compare with the gift of salvation. God's grace is the ultimate gift, and we owe Him the ultimate in thanksgiving. Let us praise the Creator for His priceless gift, and let us share the Good News with our families, with our friends, and with the world.

Christ sacrificed His life on the cross so that we might have eternal life. This gift, freely given from God's only begotten Son, is the priceless possession of everyone who accepts Him as Lord and Savior. We return our Savior's love by welcoming Him into our hearts and sharing His message and His love. When we do so, we are blessed here on earth and throughout all eternity.

You're about to begin a 100-day journey, an exploration of your faith: what it is at this moment, what it should be today, and what it can become tomorrow. During the next 100 days, you will be challenged to examine your thoughts, your priorities, your habits, and your behaviors. And you'll be challenged to strengthen your faith by learning to trust God more and more every day.

The Christian life is motivated,
not by a list of do's and don'ts,
but by the gracious outpouring of
God's love and blessing.

—

Anne Graham Lotz

The Lord's chief desire is to reveal Himself to you and, in order for Him to do that, He gives you abundant grace. The Lord gives you the experience of enjoying His presence. He touches you, and His touch is so delightful that, more than ever, you are drawn inwardly to Him.

Madame Jeanne Guyon

There is no secret that can separate you from God's love; there is no secret that can separate you from His blessings; there is no secret that is worth keeping from His grace.

Serita Ann Jakes

God's grace and power seem to reach their peak when we are at our weakest point.

Anne Graham Lotz

God is the giver, and we are the receivers. And His richest gifts are bestowed not upon those who do the greatest things, but upon those who accept His abundance and His grace.

Hannah Whitall Smith

We will never cease to need our Father—His wisdom, direction, help, and support. We will never outgrow Him. We will always need His grace.

Kay Arthur

But God, who is abundant in mercy, because of His great love that He had for us, made us alive with the Messiah even though we were dead in trespasses. By grace you are saved!

Ephesians 2:4-5 HCSB

My grace is sufficient for you, for My strength is made perfect in weakness.

2 Corinthians 12:9 NKJV

For by grace you are saved through faith, and this is not from yourselves; it is God's gift—not from works, so that no one can boast.

Ephesians 2:8-9 HCSB

And we have seen and testify that the Father has sent the Son as Savior of the world.

1 John 4:14 NKJV

TODAY'S PRAYER OF GRACE

Dear Lord, You have offered Your grace freely through Christ Jesus. I praise You for that priceless gift. Let me share the good news of Your Son with a world that desperately needs His peace, His abundance, His love, and His salvation. Amen

DAY 2

EXPERIENCING CHRIST'S LOVE

For I am persuaded that neither death nor life, nor angels nor principalities nor powers, nor things present nor things to come, nor height nor depth, nor any other created thing, shall be able to separate us from the love of God which is in Christ Jesus our Lord.

Romans 8:38-39 NKJV

How much does Christ love us? More than we, as mere mortals, can comprehend. His love is perfect and steadfast. Even though we are fallible and wayward, the Good Shepherd cares for us still. Even though we have fallen far short of the Father's commandments, Christ loves us with a power and depth that are beyond our understanding. The sacrifice that Jesus made upon the cross was made for each of us, and His love endures to the edge of eternity and beyond.

Christ is the ultimate Savior of mankind and the personal Savior of those who believe in Him. As His servants, we should place Him at the very center of our lives. And, every day that God gives us breath, we should share Christ's love and His message with a world that needs both.

Christ's love changes everything. When you accept His gift of grace, you are transformed, not only for today, but also for all eternity. If you haven't already done so, accept Jesus Christ as your Savior. He's waiting patiently for you to invite Him into your heart. Please don't make Him wait a single minute longer.

Jesus is all compassion.
He never betrays us.

—

Catherine Marshall

Jesus, my Savior, look on me, / For I am weary and oppressed; / I come to cast myself on Thee: / Thou art my Rest.

Charlotte Elliott

The love of Christ is a fierce thing. It can take the picture you have of yourself and burn it in the fire of his loving eyes, replacing it with a true masterpiece.

Sheila Walsh

It is when we come to the Lord in our nothingness, our powerlessness and our helplessness that He then enables us to love in a way which, without Him, would be absolutely impossible.

Elisabeth Elliot

Live your lives in love, the same sort of love which Christ gives us, and which He perfectly expressed when He gave Himself as a sacrifice to God.

Corrie ten Boom

Blessed assurance, Jesus is mine! O what a foretaste of glory divine!

Fanny Crosby

I am the good shepherd. The good shepherd lays down his life for the sheep.

John 10:11 HCSB

But God proves His own love for us in that while we were still sinners Christ died for us!

Romans 5:8 HCSB

No one has greater love than this, that someone would lay down his life for his friends.

John 15:13 HCSB

Who can separate us from the love of Christ? Can affliction or anguish or persecution or famine or nakedness or danger or sword? . . . No, in all these things we are more than victorious through Him who loved us.

Romans 8:35,37 HCSB

Today's Prayer of Grace

Dear Jesus, I praise You for Your love, a love that never ends. Today, I will return Your love and I will share it with the world. Amen

PRAISE HIM AND THANK HIM

Our prayers for you are always spilling over into thanksgivings. We can't quit thanking God our Father and Jesus our Messiah for you!

Colossians 1:3 MSG

Sometimes, life-here-on-earth can be complicated, demanding, and busy. When the demands of life leave us rushing from place to place with scarcely a moment to spare, we may fail to pause and say a word of thanks for all the good things we've received. But when we fail to count our blessings, we rob ourselves of the happiness, the peace, and the gratitude that should rightfully be ours.

Today, even if you're busily engaged in life, slow down long enough to start counting your blessings. You most certainly will not be able to count them all, but take a few moments to jot down as many blessings as you can. Then, give thanks to the Giver of all good things: God. His love for you is eternal, as are His gifts. And it's never too soon—or too late—to offer Him thanks.

The best way to show my gratitude to God is to accept everything, even my problems, with joy.

Mother Teresa

Thanksgiving or complaining—these words express two contrastive attitudes of the souls of God's children in regard to His dealings with them. The soul that gives thanks can find comfort in everything; the soul that complains can find comfort in nothing.

Hannah Whitall Smith

God is worthy of our praise and is pleased when we come before Him with thanksgiving.

Shirley Dobson

One reason why we don't thank God for his answer to our prayer is that frequently we don't recognize them as being answers to our prayers. We just take his bountiful supply or dramatic action for granted when it comes.

Evelyn Christenson

The game was to just find something about everything to be glad about—no matter what it was. You see, when you're hunting for the glad things, you sort of forget the other kind.

Eleanor H. Porter

Thanks be to God for His indescribable gift.

2 Corinthians 9:15 HCSB

Therefore as you have received Christ Jesus the Lord, walk in Him, rooted and built up in Him and established in the faith, just as you were taught, and overflowing with thankfulness.

Colossians 2:6-7 HCSB

Enter into His gates with thanksgiving, and into His courts with praise. Be thankful to Him, and bless His name. For the Lord is good; His mercy is everlasting, and His truth endures to all generations.

Psalm 100:4-5 NKJV

And whatever you do, in word or in deed, do everything in the name of the Lord Jesus, giving thanks to God the Father through Him.

Colossians 3:17 HCSB

TODAY'S PRAYER OF GRACE

Heavenly Father, Your gifts are greater than I can imagine. May I live each day with thanksgiving in my heart and praise on my lips. Thank You for the gift of Your Son and for the promise of eternal life. Let me share the joyous news of Jesus Christ, and let my life be a testimony to His love and His grace. Amen

SERVE HIM

*We know we love God's children if we love God
and obey his commandments.*

1 John 5:2 NLT

The teachings of Jesus are clear: We achieve greatness through service to others. But, as weak human beings, we sometimes fall short as we seek to puff ourselves up and glorify our own accomplishments. Jesus commands otherwise. He teaches us that the most esteemed men and women are not the self-congratulatory leaders of society but are instead the humblest of servants.

Today, you may feel the temptation to build yourself up in the eyes of your neighbors. Resist that temptation. Instead, serve your neighbors quietly and without fanfare. Find a need and fill it . . . humbly. Lend a helping hand and share a word of kindness . . . anonymously, for this is God's way.

As a humble servant, you will glorify yourself not before men, but before God, and that's what God intends. After all, earthly glory is fleeting: here today and all too soon gone. But, heavenly glory endures throughout eternity. So, the choice is yours: Either you can lift yourself up here on earth and be humbled in heaven, or vice versa. Choose vice versa.

God has lots of folks who intend to go to work for Him "some day." What He needs is more people who are willing to work for Him today.

Marie T. Freeman

Doing something positive toward another person is a practical approach to feeling good about yourself.

Barbara Johnson

If you want to discover your spiritual gifts, start obeying God. As you serve Him, you will find that He has given you the gifts that are necessary to follow through in obedience.

Anne Graham Lotz

God wants us to serve Him with a willing spirit, one that would choose no other way.

Beth Moore

In the very place where God has put us, whatever its limitations, whatever kind of work it may be, we may indeed serve the Lord Christ.

Elisabeth Elliot

If you want to discover
your spiritual gifts,
start obeying God.
As you serve Him,
you will find that He has
given you the gifts that are
necessary to follow through
in obedience.

—

Anne Graham Lotz

Worship the Lord your God and . . . serve Him only.

Matthew 4:10 HCSB

A person should consider us in this way: as servants of Christ and managers of God's mysteries. In this regard, it is expected of managers that each one be found faithful.

1 Corinthians 4:1-2 HCSB

If they serve Him obediently, they will end their days in prosperity and their years in happiness.

Job 36:11 HCSB

We must do the works of Him who sent Me while it is day. Night is coming when no one can work.

John 9:4 HCSB

TODAY'S PRAYER OF GRACE

Dear Lord, in weak moments, I seek to build myself up by placing myself ahead of others. But Your commandment, Father, is that I become a humble servant to those who need my encouragement, my help, and my love. Create in me a servant's heart. And, let me be a woman who follows in the footsteps of Your Son Jesus who taught us by example that to be great in Your eyes, Lord, is to serve others humbly, faithfully, and lovingly. Amen

FINDING GENUINE PEACE

*But now in Christ Jesus you who once
were far off have been brought near by the blood of Christ.
For He Himself is our peace.*

Ephesians 2:13-14 NKJV

On many occasions, our outer struggles are simply manifestations of the inner conflicts that we feel when we stray from God's path. What's needed is a refresher course in God's promise of peace. The beautiful words of John 14:27 remind us that Jesus offers peace, not as the world gives, but as He alone gives: "Peace I leave with you. My peace I give to you. I do not give to you as the world gives. Your heart must not be troubled or fearful" (HCSB).

As believers, our challenge is straightforward: we should welcome Christ's peace into our hearts and then, as best we can, share His peace with our neighbors.

Today, as a gift to yourself, to your family, and to your friends, invite Christ to preside over every aspect of your life. It's the best way to live and the surest path to peace . . . today and forever.

To know God as He really is—in His essential nature and character—is to arrive at a citadel of peace that circumstances may storm, but can never capture.

Catherine Marshall

In the center of a hurricane there is absolute quiet and peace. There is no safer place than in the center of the will of God.

Corrie ten Boom

I believe that in every time and place it is within our power to acquiesce in the will of God—and what peace it brings to do so!

Elisabeth Elliot

Prayer guards hearts and minds and causes God to bring peace out of chaos.

Beth Moore

I want first of all . . . to be at peace with myself. I want a singleness of eye, a purity of intention, a central core to my life . . . . I want, in fact—to borrow from the language of the saints—to live "in grace" as much of the time as possible.

Anne Morrow Lindbergh

These things I have spoken to you, that in Me you may have peace. In the world you will have tribulation; but be of good cheer, I have overcome the world.

John 16:33 NKJV

If your sinful nature controls your mind, there is death. But if the Holy Spirit controls your mind, there is life and peace.

Romans 8:6 NLT

And the peace of God, which surpasses all understanding, will guard your hearts and minds through Christ Jesus. Finally, brethren, whatever things are true, whatever things are noble, whatever things are just, whatever things are pure, whatever things are lovely, whatever things are of good report, if there is any virtue and if there is anything praiseworthy—meditate on these things.

Philippians 4:7-8 NKJV

TODAY'S PRAYER OF GRACE

Dear Lord, let me accept the peace and abundance that You offer through Your Son Jesus. You are the Giver of all things good, Father, and You give me peace when I draw close to You. Help me to trust Your will, to follow Your commands, and to accept Your peace, today and forever. Amen

His Grace Is Sufficient for Difficult Days

We are troubled on every side, yet not distressed;
we are perplexed, but not in despair. . . .

2 Corinthians 4:8 KJV

As we travel the roads of life, all of us are confronted with streets that seem to be dead ends. When we do, we may become discouraged. After all, we live in a society where expectations can be high and demands even higher.

If you find yourself enduring difficult circumstances, remember that God remains in His heaven. If you become discouraged with the direction of your day or your life, turn your thoughts and prayers to Him. He is a God of possibility, not negativity. He will guide you through your difficulties and beyond them. And then, with a renewed spirit of optimism and hope, you can thank the Giver of all things good for gifts that are simply too profound to fully understand and for treasures that are too numerous to count.

If God sends us on stony paths, he provides strong shoes.

Corrie ten Boom

Often God shuts a door in our face so that he can open the door through which he wants us to go.

Catherine Marshall

This hard place in which you perhaps find yourself is the very place in which God is giving you opportunity to look only to Him, to spend time in prayer, and to learn long-suffering, gentleness, meekness—in short, to learn the depths of the love that Christ Himself has poured out on all of us.

Elisabeth Elliot

We all go through pain and sorrow, but the presence of God, like a warm, comforting blanket, can shield us and protect us, and allow the deep inner joy to surface, even in the most devastating circumstances.

Barbara Johnson

Recently I've been learning that life comes down to this: God is in everything. Regardless of what difficulties I am experiencing at the moment, or what things aren't as I would like them to be, I look at the circumstances and say, "Lord, what are you trying to teach me?"

Catherine Marshall

Often the trials we mourn
are really gateways into
the good things we long for.

———

Hannah Whitall Smith

We also have joy with our troubles, because we know that these troubles produce patience. And patience produces character, and character produces hope.

Romans 5:3-4 NCV

The LORD also will be a stronghold for the oppressed, a stronghold in times of trouble.

Psalm 9:9 NASB

Don't fret or worry. Instead of worrying, pray. Let petitions and praises shape your worries into prayers, letting God know your concerns. Before you know it, a sense of God's wholeness, everything coming together for good, will come and settle you down. It's wonderful what happens when Christ displaces worry at the center of your life.

Philippians 4:6-7 MSG

Today's Prayer of Grace

Heavenly Father, You are my strength and my refuge. As I journey through this day, I know that I may encounter disappointments and losses. When I am troubled, let me turn to You. Keep me steady, Lord, and renew a right spirit inside of me this day and forever. Amen

DREAMING BIG DREAMS

When dreams come true, there is life and joy.
Proverbs 13:12 NLT

A re you willing to entertain the possibility that God has big plans in store for you? Hopefully so. Yet sometimes, especially if you've recently experienced a life-altering disappointment, you may find it difficult to envision a brighter future for yourself and your family. If so, it's time to reconsider your own capabilities . . . and God's.

Your Heavenly Father created you with unique gifts and untapped talents; your job is to tap them. When you do, you'll begin to feel an increasing sense of confidence in yourself and in your future.

It takes courage to dream big dreams. You will discover that courage when you do three things: accept the past, trust God to handle the future, and make the most of the time He has given you today.

Nothing is too difficult for God, and no dreams are too big for Him—not even yours. So start living—and dreaming—accordingly.

The future belongs to those who believe in the beauty of their dreams.

Eleanor Roosevelt

The future lies all before us. Shall it only be a slight advance upon what we usually do? Ought it not to be a bound, a leap forward to altitudes of endeavor and success undreamed of before?

Annie Armstrong

Allow your dreams a place in your prayers and plans. God-given dreams can help you move into the future He is preparing for you.

Barbara Johnson

Always stay connected to people and seek out things that bring you joy. Dream with abandon. Pray confidently.

Barbara Johnson

God created us with an overwhelming desire to soar. He designed us to be tremendously productive and "to mount up with wings like eagles," realistically dreaming of what He can do with our potential.

Carol Kent

Our dreams are who we are.

Barbara Sher

Live full lives, full in the fullness of God. God can do anything, you know—far more than you could ever imagine or guess or request in your wildest dreams! He does it not by pushing us around but by working within us, his Spirit deeply and gently within us.

Ephesians 3:19-20 MSG

I came so they can have real and eternal life, more and better life than they ever dreamed of.

John 10:10 MSG

It is pleasant to see dreams come true, but fools will not turn from evil to attain them.

Proverbs 13:19 NLT

Where there is no vision, the people perish. . . .

Proverbs 29:18 KJV

TODAY'S PRAYER OF GRACE

Dear Lord, give me the courage to dream and the faithfulness to trust in Your perfect plan. When I am worried or weary, give me strength for today and hope for tomorrow. Keep me mindful of Your healing power, Your infinite love, and Your eternal salvation. Amen

PRAISE HIM FOR YOUR TALENTS

God has given gifts to each of you from his great variety of spiritual gifts. Manage them well so that God's generosity can flow through you.

1 Peter 4:10 NLT

Your talents, resources, and opportunities are all gifts from the Giver of all things good. And the best way to say "Thank You" for these gifts is to use them.

Do you have a particular talent? Hone your skill and use it. Do you possess financial resources? Share them. Have you been blessed by a particular opportunity, or have you experienced unusual good fortune? Use your good fortune to help others.

When you share the gifts God has given you—and when you share them freely and without fanfare—you invite God to bless you more and more. So today, do yourself and the world a favor: be a faithful steward of your talents and treasures. And then prepare yourself for even greater blessings that are sure to come.

The Lord has abundantly blessed me all of my life. I'm not trying to pay Him back for all of His wonderful gifts; I just realize that He gave them to me to give away.

Lisa Whelchel

Not everyone possesses boundless energy or a conspicuous talent. We are not equally blessed with great intellect or physical beauty or emotional strength. But we have all been given the same ability to be faithful.

Gigi Graham Tchividjian

It is the definition of joy to be able to offer back to God the essence of what he's placed in you, be that creativity or a love of ideas or a compassionate heart or the gift of hospitality.

Paula Rinehart

Yes, we need to acknowledge our weaknesses, to confess our sins. But if we want to be active, productive participants in the realm of God, we also need to recognize our gifts, to appreciate our strengths, to build on the abilities God has given us. We need to balance humility with confidence.

Penelope Stokes

God has given you special talents—now it's your turn to give them back to God.

Marie T. Freeman

According to the grace given to us, we have different gifts: If prophecy, use it according to the standard of faith; if service, in service; if teaching, in teaching; if exhorting, in exhortation; giving, with generosity; leading, with diligence; showing mercy, with cheerfulness.

Romans 12:6-8 HCSB

Do not neglect the gift that is in you.

1 Timothy 4:14 HCSB

So he who had received five talents came and brought five other talents, saying, "Lord, you delivered to me five talents; look, I have gained five more talents besides them." His lord said to him, "Well done, good and faithful servant; you were faithful over a few things, I will make you ruler over many things. Enter into the joy of your lord."

Matthew 25:20-21 NKJV

Today's Prayer of Grace

Father, You have given me abilities to be used for the glory of Your kingdom. Give me the courage and the perseverance to use those talents. Keep me mindful that all my gifts come from You, Lord. Let me be Your faithful, humble servant, and let me give You all the glory and all the praise. Amen

THE GIFT OF CHEERFULNESS

Be cheerful. Keep things in good repair. Keep your spirits up.
Think in harmony. Be agreeable. Do all that,
and the God of love and peace will be with you for sure.

2 Corinthians 13:11 MSG

O n some days, as every woman knows, it's hard to be cheerful. Sometimes, as the demands of the world increase and our energy sags, we feel less like "cheering up" and more like "tearing up." But even in our darkest hours, we can turn to God, and He will give us comfort.

Few things in life are more sad, or, for that matter, more absurd, than a grumpy Christian. Christ promises us lives of abundance and joy, but He does not force His joy upon us. We must claim His joy for ourselves, and when we do, Jesus, in turn, fills our spirits with His power and His love.

How can we receive from Christ the joy that is rightfully ours? By giving Him what is rightfully His: our hearts and our souls.

When we earnestly commit ourselves to the Savior of mankind, when we place Jesus at the center of our lives and trust Him as our personal Savior, He will transform us, not just for today, but for all eternity. Then we, as God's children, can share Christ's joy and His message with a world that needs both.

When we bring sunshine into the lives of others, we're warmed by it ourselves. When we spill a little happiness, it splashes on us.

Barbara Johnson

A sad nun is a bad nun; I am more afraid of one unhappy sister than of a crowd of evil spirits.

St. Teresa of Avila

Cheerfulness prepares a glorious mind for all the noblest acts of religion—love, adoration, praise, and every union with our God.

St. Elizabeth Ann Seton

We may run, walk, stumble, drive, or fly, but let us never lose sight of the reason for the journey, or miss a chance to see a rainbow on the way.

Gloria Gaither

Make each day useful and cheerful
and prove that you know
the worth of time by employing
it well. Then youth will be happy,
old age without regret,
and life a beautiful success.

—

Louisa May Alcott

A merry heart does good, like medicine.

Proverbs 17:22 NKJV

Is anyone cheerful? He should sing praises.

James 5:13 HCSB

Bright eyes cheer the heart; good news strengthens the bones.

Proverbs 15:30 HCSB

A cheerful heart has a continual feast.

Proverbs 15:15 HCSB

Today's Prayer of Grace

Dear Lord, You have given me so many reasons to celebrate. Today, let me choose an attitude of cheerfulness. Let me be a joyful Christian, Lord, quick to smile and slow to anger. And, let me share Your goodness with all whom I meet so that Your love might shine in me and through me. Amen

Praising God for His Word

Every word of God is flawless;
he is a shield to those who take refuge in him.

Proverbs 30:5 NIV

God's Word is unlike any other book. The Bible is a roadmap for life here on earth and for life eternal. As Christians, we are called upon to study God's Holy Word, to trust His Word, to follow its commandments, and to share its Good News with the world.

The words of Matthew 4:4 remind us that, "Man shall not live by bread alone but by every word that proceedeth out of the mouth of God" (KJV). As believers, we must study the Bible and meditate upon its meaning for our lives. Otherwise, we deprive ourselves of a priceless gift from our Creator.

Warren Wiersbe observed, "When the child of God looks into the Word of God, he sees the Son of God. And, he is transformed by the Spirit of God to share in the glory of God." God's Holy Word is, indeed, a transforming, life-changing, one-of-a-kind treasure. And, a passing acquaintance with the Good Book is insufficient for Christians who seek to obey God's Word and to understand His will. After all, man does not live by bread alone . . .

Obedience is a foundational stepping stone on the path of God's Will.

Elizabeth George

Study the Bible and observe how the persons behaved and how God dealt with them. There is explicit teaching on every condition of life.

Corrie ten Boom

Unless we form the habit of going to the Bible in bright moments as well as in trouble, we cannot fully respond to its consolations because we lack equilibrium between light and darkness.

Helen Keller

We can't stand before God on the day of judgment and explain that our incredible ignorance is our pastor's fault. It is our responsibility to access God's Word for ourselves.

Sheila Walsh

Man shall not live by bread alone, but by every word that proceeds from the mouth of God.

Matthew 4:4 NKJV

Blessed are those who hunger and thirst for righteousness, for they will be filled.

Matthew 5:6 NIV

For the word of God is quick, and powerful, and sharper than any two-edged sword, piercing even to the dividing asunder of soul and spirit, and of the joints and marrow, and is a discerner of the thoughts and intents of the heart.

Hebrews 4:12 KJV

Jesus answered and said unto him, If a man love me, he will keep my words: and my Father will love him, and we will come unto him, and make our abode with him.

John 14:23 KJV

TODAY'S PRAYER OF GRACE

Dear Lord, the Bible is Your gift to me; thank You. When I stray from Your Holy Word, Father, I suffer. But, when I place Your Word at the very center of my life, I am protected and blessed. Make me a faithful student of Your Word today and every day. Amen

TRUSTING YOUR CONSCIENCE

I will maintain my righteousness and never let go of it;
my conscience will not reproach me as long as I live.

Job 27:6 NIV

Few things in life torment us more than a guilty conscience. And, few things in life provide more contentment than the knowledge that we are obeying God's commandments. A clear conscience is one of the rewards we earn when we obey God's Word and follow His will. When we follow God's will and accept His gift of salvation, our earthly rewards are never-ceasing, and our heavenly rewards are everlasting.

Billy Graham correctly observed, "Most of us follow our conscience as we follow a wheelbarrow. We push it in front of us in the direction we want to go." If that describes you, then here's a word of warning: both you and your wheelbarrow are headed for trouble.

You can sometimes keep secrets from other people, but you can never keep secrets from God. God knows what you think and what you do. And if you want to please Him, you must start with good intentions, a pure heart, and a clear conscience.

If you sincerely wish to walk with God, follow His commandments. When you do, your character will take care of itself . . . and so will your conscience. Then, as you journey through life, you won't need to look over your shoulder to see who—besides God—is watching.

If you listen to your conscience, it will serve you as no other friend you'll ever know.

Loretta Young

Whatever weakens your reason, impairs the tenderness of your conscience, obscures your sense of God, or removes your relish for spiritual things—that is sin to you.

Susanna Wesley

There is a balance to be maintained in situations. That balance is the Holy Spirit within us to guide us into the truth of each situation and circumstance in which we find ourselves. He will provide us the wisdom to know when we are to be adaptable and adjustable and when we are to take a firm stand and be immovable.

Joyce Meyer

While conscience is our friend,
all is at peace;
however once it is offended,
farewell to a tranquil mind.

—

Lady Mary Wortley Montagu

So I strive always to keep my conscience clear before God and man.

Acts 24:16 NIV

Let us draw near to God with a sincere heart in full assurance of faith, having our hearts sprinkled to cleanse us from a guilty conscience and having our bodies washed with pure water.

Hebrews 10:22 NIV

Now the goal of our instruction is love from a pure heart, a good conscience, and a sincere faith.

1 Timothy 1:5 HCSB

Do not conform any longer to the pattern of this world, but be transformed by the renewing of your mind. Then you will be able to test and approve what God's will is—his good, pleasing and perfect will.

Romans 12:2 NIV

TODAY'S PRAYER OF GRACE

Dear Lord, You speak to me through the gift of Your Holy Word. And, Father, You speak to me through that still small voice that tells me right from wrong. Let me follow Your way, Lord, and, in these quiet moments, show me Your plan for this day, that I might serve You. Amen

Finding Contentment

But godliness with contentment is a great gain.

1 Timothy 6:6 HCSB

Everywhere we turn, or so it seems, the world promises us contentment and happiness. We are bombarded by messages offering us the "good life" if only we will purchase products and services that are designed to provide happiness, success, and contentment. But the contentment that the world offers is fleeting and incomplete. Thankfully, the contentment that God offers is all encompassing and everlasting.

Happiness depends less upon our circumstances than upon our thoughts. When we turn our thoughts to God, to His gifts, and to His glorious creation, we experience the joy that God intends for His children. But, when we focus on the negative aspects of life—or when we disobey God's commandments—we cause ourselves needless suffering.

Do you sincerely want to be a contented Christian? Then set your mind and your heart upon God's love and His grace. Seek first the salvation that is available through a personal relationship with Jesus Christ, and then claim the joy, the contentment, and the spiritual abundance that God offers His children.

Oh, what a happy soul I am, although I cannot see! I am resolved that in this world, contented I will be.

Fanny Crosby

If I could just hang in there, being faithful to my own tasks, God would make me joyful and content. The responsibility is mine, but the power is His.

Peg Rankin

The key to contentment is to consider. Consider who you are and be satisfied with that. Consider what you have and be satisfied with that. Consider what God's doing and be satisfied with that.

Luci Swindoll

If God chooses to remain silent, faith is content.

Ruth Bell Graham

When you accept rather than fight your circumstances, even though you don't understand them, you open your heart's gate to God's love, peace, joy, and contentment.

Amy Carmichael

I have learned to be content in whatever circumstances I am.

Philippians 4:11 HCSB

The LORD will give strength to His people; The LORD will bless His people with peace.

Psalm 29:11 NKJV

A tranquil heart is life to the body, but jealousy is rottenness to the bones.

Proverbs 14:30 HCSB

How priceless is your unfailing love! Both high and low among men find refuge in the shadow of your wings. They feast on the abundance of your house; you give them drink from your river of delights. For with you is the fountain of life; in your light we see light.

Psalm 36:7-9 NIV

TODAY'S PRAYER OF GRACE

Dear Lord, You offer me contentment, and I praise You for that gift. Today, I will accept Your peace. I will trust Your Word, I will follow Your commandments, and I will welcome the peace of Jesus into my heart, today and forever. Amen

Ask Him

Keep asking, and it will be given to you. Keep searching,
and you will find. Keep knocking, and the door will be
opened to you. For everyone who asks receives,
and the one who searches finds, and to the one who knocks,
the door will be opened.

Matthew 7:7-8 HCSB

Are you a woman who confidently asks God to move mountains, or do you timidly ask Him to push around a few molehills? God is perfectly capable of moving either molehills or mountains, so it's up to you to decide whether you want His help on big projects or tiny ones.

How often do you ask for God's help? Occasionally? Intermittently? Whenever you experience a crisis? Hopefully not. Hopefully, you have developed the habit of asking for God's assistance early and often. And hopefully, you have learned to seek His guidance in every aspect of your life.

God has promised that when you ask for His help, He will not withhold it. So ask. Ask Him to meet the needs of your day. Ask Him for wisdom. Ask Him to lead you, to protect you, and to correct you. And don't hesitate to ask Him to do big things in your own life and in the lives of your loved ones.

God stands at the door and waits. When you knock on His door, He answers. Your task, of course, is to seek His guidance prayerfully, confidently, and often.

When will we realize that we're not troubling God with our questions and concerns? His heart is open to hear us— His touch nearer than our next thought—as if no one in the world existed but us. Our very personal God wants to hear from us personally.

Gigi Graham Tchividjian

Often I have made a request of God with earnest pleadings even backed up with Scripture, only to have Him say "No" because He had something better in store.

Ruth Bell Graham

By asking in Jesus' name, we're making a request not only in His authority, but also for His interests and His benefit.

Shirley Dobson

When you ask God
to do something, don't ask timidly;
put your whole heart into it.

—

Marie T. Freeman

So I say to you, keep asking, and it will be given to you. Keep searching, and you will find. Keep knocking, and the door will be opened to you.

Luke 11:9 HCSB

What father among you, if his son asks for a fish, will, instead of a fish, give him a snake? Or if he asks for an egg, will give him a scorpion? If you then, who are evil, know how to give good gifts to your children, how much more will the heavenly Father give the Holy Spirit to those who ask Him?

Luke 11:11-13 HCSB

And in that day you will ask Me nothing. Most assuredly, I say to you, whatever you ask the Father in My name He will give you. Until now you have asked nothing in My name. Ask, and you will receive, that your joy may be full.

John 16:23-24 NKJV

TODAY'S PRAYER OF GRACE

Lord, when I have questions or fears, I will turn to You. When I am weak, I will seek Your strength. When I am discouraged, Father, I will be mindful of Your love and Your grace. I will ask You for the things I need, Father, and I will trust Your answers, today and forever. Amen

TRUST HIS PROMISES

This is my comfort in my affliction:
Your promise has given me life.
Psalm 119:50 HCSB

God's promises are found in a book like no other: the Holy Bible. The Bible is a roadmap for life here on earth and for life eternal. As Christians, we are called upon to trust its promises, to follow its commandments, and to share its Good News.

As believers, we must study the Bible daily and meditate upon its meaning for our lives. Otherwise, we deprive ourselves of a priceless gift from our Creator. God's Holy Word is, indeed, a transforming, life-changing, one-of-a-kind treasure. And, a passing acquaintance with the Good Book is insufficient for Christians who seek to obey God's Word and to understand His will.

God has made promises to mankind and to you. God's promises never fail and they never grow old. You must trust those promises and share them with your family, with your friends, and with the world.

Joy is not mere happiness. Nor does joy spring from a life of ease, comfort, or peaceful circumstances. Joy is the soul's buoyant response to a God of promise, presence, and power.

Susan Lenzkes

We have ample evidence that the Lord is able to guide. The promises cover every imaginable situation. All we need to do is to take the hand he stretches out.

Elisabeth Elliot

Brother, is your faith looking upward today? / Trust in the promise of the Savior. / Sister, is the light shining bright on your way? / Trust in the promise of thy Lord.

Fanny Crosby

We get into trouble when we think we know what to do and we stop asking God if we're doing it.

Stormie Omartian

Fear and doubt are conquered by a faith that rejoices. And faith can rejoice because the promises of God are as certain as God Himself.

Kay Arthur

The meaning of hope isn't just
some flimsy wishing.
It's a firm confidence in
God's promises—that he will
ultimately set things right.

—

Sheila Walsh

Whatever God has promised gets stamped with the Yes of Jesus. In him, this is what we preach and pray, the great Amen, God's Yes and our Yes together, gloriously evident.

2 Corinthians 1:20 MSG

Let's keep a firm grip on the promises that keep us going. He always keeps his word.

Hebrews 10:23 MSG

God also bound himself with an oath, so that those who received the promise could be perfectly sure that he would never change his mind. So God has given us both his promise and his oath. These two things are unchangeable because it is impossible for God to lie. Therefore, we who have fled to him for refuge can take new courage, for we can hold on to his promise with confidence.

Hebrews 6:17-18 NLT

TODAY'S PRAYER OF GRACE

Lord, Your Holy Word contains promises, and I will trust them. I will use the Bible as my guide, and I will trust You, Lord, to speak to me through Your Holy Spirit and through Your Holy Word, this day and forever. Amen

THE BALANCING ACT

Come to Me, all you who labor and are heavy laden, and
I will give you rest. Take My yoke upon you and learn from
Me, for I am gentle and lowly in heart, and you will find rest
for your souls. For My yoke is easy and My burden is light.
Matthew 11:28-30 NKJV

Face facts: life is a delicate balancing act, a tightrope walk with over-commitment on one side and under-commitment on the other. And it's up to each of us to walk carefully on that rope, not falling prey to pride (which causes us to attempt too much) or to fear (which causes us to attempt too little).

God's Word promises us the possibility of abundance (John 10:10). And we are far more likely to experience that abundance when we lead balanced lives.

Are you doing too much—or too little? If so, it's time to have a little chat with God. And if you listen carefully to His instructions, you will strive to achieve a more balanced life, a life that's right for you and your loved ones. When you do, everybody wins.

Does God care about all the responsibilities we have to juggle in our daily lives? Of course. But he cares more that our lives demonstrate balance, the ability to discern what is essential and give ourselves fully to it.

Penelope Stokes

Always remember that we can learn to control our weaknesses through the power of the Holy Spirit and in doing so become well-balanced individuals who cannot be controlled by Satan.

Joyce Meyer

When I feel like circumstances are spiraling downward in my life, God taught me that whether I'm right side up or upside down, I need to turn those circumstances over to Him. He is the only one who can bring balance into my life.

Carole Lewis

To do too much is as dangerous as to do nothing at all. Both modes prevent us from savoring our moments. One causes me to rush right past the best of life without recognizing or basking in it, and the other finds me sitting quietly as life rushes past me.

Patsy Clairmont

But those who wait on the Lord shall renew their strength; they shall mount up with wings like eagles, they shall run and not be weary, they shall walk and not faint.

Isaiah 40:31 NKJV

Now it happened as they went that He entered a certain village; and a certain woman named Martha welcomed Him into her house. And she had a sister called Mary, who also sat at Jesus' feet and heard His word. But Martha was distracted with much serving, and she approached Him and said, "Lord, do You not care that my sister has left me to serve alone? Therefore tell her to help me." And Jesus answered and said to her, "Martha, Martha, you are worried and troubled about many things. But one thing is needed, and Mary has chosen that good part, which will not be taken away from her."

Luke 10:38-42 NKJV

TODAY'S PRAYER OF GRACE

I thanks You, Father, for Your blessings. Keep me mindful of Your gifts as I find contentment and balance. Let Your priorities be my priorities, and when I have done my best, give me the wisdom to place my faith and my trust in You. Amen

DAY 16

LIVING WITH YOUR BELIEFS

For the kingdom of God is not in talk but in power.
1 Corinthians 4:20 HCSB

In describing our beliefs, our actions are far better descriptors than our words. Yet far too many of us spend more energy talking about our beliefs than living by them—with predictably poor results.

As believers, we must beware: Our actions should always give credence to the changes that Christ can make in the lives of those who walk with Him.

Your beliefs shape your values, and your values shape your life. Is your life a clearly crafted picture book of your creed? And do you weave your beliefs into the very fabric of your day. If you do, God will honor your good works, and your good works will honor God.

If you seek to be a responsible believer, you must realize that it is never enough to hear the instructions of God; you must also live by them. And it is never enough to wait idly by while others do God's work here on earth. You, too, must act.

Doing God's work is a responsibility that every Christian (including you) should bear. And when you do, your loving Heavenly Father will reward your efforts with a bountiful harvest.

You can better understand the 23rd Psalm when you are acquainted with The Shepherd.

Anonymous

As parents, we must be convinced of our beliefs. We must know where we stand, so that our children will know where they stand.

Kim Boyce

What God asks of us is both simpler and more profound than adherence to a system of beliefs or following a set of rules. He asks us to walk with him through the blood and guts of our real experience in an honest pilgrimage where we let him show us what real strength, and real love, are all about.

Paula Rinehart

Jesus taught that the evidence that confirms our leaps of faith comes after we risk believing, not before.

Gloria Gaither

If all things are possible with God,
then all things are possible to him
who believes in him.

—

Corrie ten Boom

Everyone who believes that Jesus is the Messiah has been born of God, and everyone who loves the parent also loves his child.

1 John 5:1 HCSB

I know whom I have believed and am persuaded that He is able to guard what has been entrusted to me until that day.

2 Timothy 1:12 HCSB

Then He said to Thomas, "Put your finger here and observe My hands. Reach out your hand and put it into My side. Don't be an unbeliever, but a believer."

John 20:27 HCSB

Then Jesus told the centurion, "Go. As you have believed, let it be done for you." And his servant was cured that very moment.

Matthew 8:13 HCSB

TODAY'S PRAYER OF GRACE

Heavenly Father, I believe in You, and I believe in Your Word. Help me to live in such a way that my actions validate my beliefs—and let the glory be Yours forever. Amen

DAY 17

SPIRITUAL GROWTH

*Grow in grace and understanding of our Master and Savior,
Jesus Christ. Glory to the Master, now and forever! Yes!*
2 Peter 3:18 MSG

Are you continuing to grow in your love and knowledge of the Lord, or are you "satisfied" with the current state of your spiritual health? Your relationship with God is ongoing; it unfolds day by day, and it offers countless opportunities to grow closer to Him . . . or not. As each new day unfolds, you are confronted with a wide range of decisions: how you will behave, where you will direct your thoughts, with whom you will associate, and what you will choose to worship. These choices, along with many others like them, are yours and yours alone. How you choose determines how your relationship with God will unfold.

Hopefully, you're determined to make yourself a growing Christian. Your Savior deserves no less, and neither, by the way, do you.

Growing up in Christ is surely the most difficult, courageous, exhilarating, and eternally important work any of us will ever do.

Susan Lenzkes

You are either becoming more like Christ every day or you're becoming less like Him. There is no neutral position in the Lord.

Stormie Omartian

There is nothing more important than understanding God's truth and being changed by it, so why are we so casual about accepting the popular theology of the moment without checking it out for ourselves? God has given us a mind so that we can learn and grow. As his people, we have a great responsibility and wonderful privilege of growing in our understanding of him.

Sheila Walsh

If all struggles and sufferings were eliminated, the spirit would no more reach maturity than would the child.

Elisabeth Elliot

We set our eyes on the finish line, forgetting the past, and straining toward the mark of spiritual maturity and fruitfulness.

Vonette Bright

For this reason also, since the day we heard this, we haven't stopped praying for you. We are asking that you may be filled with the knowledge of His will in all wisdom and spiritual understanding.

Colossians 1:9 HCSB

I want their hearts to be encouraged and joined together in love, so that they may have all the riches of assured understanding, and have the knowledge of God's mystery—Christ.

Colossians 2:2 HCSB

For You, O God, have tested us; You have refined us as silver is refined. You brought us into the net; You laid affliction on our backs. You have caused men to ride over our heads; we went through fire and through water; but You brought us out to rich fulfillment.

Psalm 66:10–12 NKJV

TODAY'S PRAYER OF GRACE

Dear Lord, thank You for the opportunity to walk with Your Son. And, thank You for the opportunity to grow closer to You each day. I thank You for the person I am and for the person I can become. Amen

Day 18

STRENGTH FOR TODAY

Search for the Lord and for His strength;
seek His face always.
Psalm 105:4-5 HCSB

God's love and support never changes. From the cradle to the grave, God has promised to give you the strength to meet any challenge. God has promised to lift you up and guide your steps if you let Him. God has promised that when you entrust your life to Him completely and without reservation, He will give you the courage to face any trial and the wisdom to live in His righteousness.

God's hand uplifts those who turn their hearts and prayers to Him. Will you count yourself among that number? Will you accept God's peace and wear God's armor against the temptations and distractions of our dangerous world? If you do, you can live courageously and optimistically, knowing that you have been forever touched by the loving, unfailing, uplifting hand of God.

The miraculous thing about being a family is that in the last analysis, we are each dependent of one another and God, woven together by mercy given and mercy received.

Barbara Johnson

No matter how heavy the burden, daily strength is given, so I expect we need not give ourselves any concern as to what the outcome will be. We must simply go forward.

Annie Armstrong

When we spend time with Christ, He supplies us with strength and encourages us in the pursuit of His ways.

Elizabeth George

When we reach the end of our strength, wisdom, and personal resources, we enter into the beginning of his glorious provisions.

Patsy Clairmont

If your every human plan and calculation has miscarried, if, one by one, human props have been knocked out . . . take heart. God is trying to get a message through to you, and the message is: "Stop depending on inadequate human resources. Let me handle the matter."

Catherine Marshall

Living by faith requires patience,
for the one who lives by faith
becomes dependent upon God.

—

Kay Arthur

And He said to me, "My grace is sufficient for you, for My strength is made perfect in weakness."

2 Corinthians 12:9 NKJV

You, therefore, my child, be strong in the grace that is in Christ Jesus.

2 Timothy 2:1 HCSB

The Lord is my strength and my song; He has become my salvation.

Exodus 15:2 HCSB

He gives strength to the weary and strengthens the powerless.

Isaiah 40:29 HCSB

Today's Prayer of Grace

Dear Lord, I will turn to You for strength. When my responsibilities seem overwhelming, I will trust You to give me courage and perspective. Today and every day, I will look to You as the ultimate source of my hope, my strength, my peace, and my salvation. Amen

DAY 19

DEFINING SUCCESS

*If you do not stand firm in your faith,
then you will not stand at all.*
Isaiah 7:9 HCSB

How do you define success? Do you define it as the accumulation of material possessions or the adulation of your neighbors? If so, you need to reorder your priorities. Genuine success has little to do with fame or fortune; it has everything to do with God's gift of love and His promise of salvation.

If you have accepted Christ as your personal Savior, you are already a towering success in the eyes of God, but there is still more that you can do. Your task—as a believer who has been touched by the Creator's grace—is to accept the spiritual abundance and peace that He offers through the person of His Son. Then, you can share the healing message of God's love and His abundance with a world that desperately needs both. When you do, you have reached the pinnacle of success.

Winners see an answer for every problem; losers see a problem in every answer.

Barbara Johnson

Success isn't the key. Faithfulness is.

Joni Eareckson Tada

We can be victorious, but only if we walk with God.

Beth Moore

Nothing I can do will make me special. No awards I can earn will make me a better person. The taproot of my being grows in the rich soil of the being of Christ instead of in the shifting sands of worldly accomplishment.

Leslie Williams

People judge us by the success of our efforts. God looks at the efforts themselves.

Charlotte Brontë

It is no exaggeration to say that a strong postive self-image is the best possible preparation for success in life.

Joyce Brothers

Success, success to you, and success to those who help you, for your God will help you. . . .

1 Chronicles 12:18 NIV

But as for you, be strong and do not give up, for your work will be rewarded.

2 Chronicles 15:7 NIV

Let us not become weary in doing good, for at the proper time we will reap a harvest if we do not give up.

Galatians 6:9 NIV

You need to persevere so that when you have done the will of God, you will receive what he has promised.

Hebrews 10:36 NIV

TODAY'S PRAYER OF GRACE

Dear Lord, let Your priorities be my priorities. Let Your will be my will. Let Your Word be my guide, and keep me mindful that genuine success is a result, not of the world's approval, but of Your approval. Amen

LIVING COURAGEOUSLY

So do not fear, for I am with you; do not be dismayed,
for I am your God. I will strengthen you and help you;
I will uphold you with my righteous right hand.

Isaiah 41:10 NIV

Christian women have every reason to live courageously. After all, the final battle has already been won on the cross at Calvary. But even dedicated followers of Christ may find their courage tested by the inevitable disappointments and fears that visit the lives of believers and non-believers alike.

When you find yourself worried about the challenges of today or the uncertainties of tomorrow, you must ask yourself whether or not you are ready to place your concerns and your life in God's all-powerful, all-knowing, all-loving hands. If the answer to that question is yes—as it should be—then you can draw courage today from the source of strength that never fails: your Heavenly Father.

What is courage? It is the ability to be strong in trust, in conviction, in obedience. To be courageous is to step out in faith—to trust and obey, no matter what.

Kay Arthur

God did away with all my fear. It was time for someone to stand up—or in my case, sit down. So I refused to move.

Rosa Parks

Just as courage is faith in good, so discouragement is faith in evil, and, while courage opens the door to good, discouragement opens it to evil.

Hannah Whitall Smith

With each new experience of letting God be in control, we gain courage and reinforcement for daring to do it again and again.

Gloria Gaither

Courage is the price that life exacts for granting peace. The soul that knows it not knows no release from little things.

Amelia Earhart

Courage is not the absence
of fear, but rather the judgment
that something else is more
important than fear.

—

Ambrose Redmoon

Be strong and courageous, and do the work. Don't be afraid or discouraged, for the Lord God, my God, is with you. He won't leave you or forsake you.

1 Chronicles 28:20 HCSB

But when Jesus heard it, He answered him, "Don't be afraid. Only believe."

Luke 8:50 HCSB

For God has not given us a spirit of fearfulness, but one of power, love, and sound judgment.

2 Timothy 1:7 HCSB

Be alert, stand firm in the faith, be brave and strong.

1 Corinthians 16:13 HCSB

TODAY'S PRAYER OF GRACE

Lord, sometimes, this world can be a fearful place, but You have promised me that You are with me always. Today, Lord, I will live courageously as I place my trust in Your everlasting power and my faith in Your everlasting love. Amen

Day 21

MAKING
THE RIGHT DECISIONS

Now if any of you lacks wisdom, he should ask God,
who gives to all generously and without criticizing,
and it will be given to him.

James 1:5 HCSB

Some decisions are easy to make because the consequences of those decisions are small. When the person behind the counter asks, "Want fries with that?" the necessary response requires little thought because the aftermath of that decision is relatively unimportant.

Some decisions, on the other hand, are big . . . very big. If you're facing one of those big decisions, here are some things you can do: 1. Gather as much information as you can: don't expect to get all the facts—that's impossible— but get as many facts as you can in a reasonable amount of time. (Proverbs 24:3-4) 2. Don't be too impulsive: If you have time to make a decision, use that time to make a good decision. (Proverbs 19:2) 3. Rely on the advice of trusted friends and mentors. Proverbs 1:5 makes it clear: "A wise man will hear and increase learning, and a man of understanding will attain wise counsel" (NKJV). 4. Pray for guidance. When you seek it, He will give it. (Luke 11:9) 5. Trust the quiet inner voice of your conscience: Treat your conscience as you would a trusted advisor. (Luke 17:21) 6. When the time for action arrives, act. Procrastination is the enemy of progress; don't let it defeat you. (James 1:22)

People who can never quite seem to make up their minds usually make themselves miserable. So when in doubt, be decisive. It's the decent way to live.

There may be no trumpet sound
or loud applause when we make
a right decision,
just a calm sense of resolution and peace.

—

Gloria Gaither

The Reference Point for the Christian is the Bible. All values, judgments, and attitudes must be gauged in relationship to this Reference Point.

Ruth Bell Graham

The location of your affections will drive the direction of your decisions.

Lisa Bevere

The principle of making no decision without prayer keeps me from rushing in and committing myself before I consult God.

Elizabeth George

If you are struggling to make some difficult decisions right now that aren't specifically addressed in the Bible, don't make a choice based on what's right for someone else. You are the Lord's and He will make sure you do what's right.

Lisa Whelchel

No trumpets sound when the important decisions of our lives are made. Destiny is made known silently.

Agnes DeMille

I have set before you life and death, blessing and curse. Choose life so that you and your descendants may live, love the Lord your God, obey Him, and remain faithful to Him. For He is your life, and He will prolong your life in the land the Lord swore to give to your fathers Abraham, Isaac, and Jacob.

Deuteronomy 30:19-20 HCSB

Ignorant zeal is worthless; haste makes waste.

Proverbs 19:2 MSG

But Daniel purposed in his heart that he would not defile himself. . . .

Daniel 1:8 KJV

But seek first the kingdom of God and His righteousness, and all these things will be provided for you.

Matthew 6:33 HCSB

TODAY'S PRAYER OF GRACE

Dear Lord, today I will focus my thoughts on Your will for my life. I will strive to make decisions that are pleasing to You, and I will strive to follow in the footsteps of Your Son. Amen

What's Really Important

Don't be obsessed with getting more material things.
Be relaxed with what you have.

Hebrews 13:5 MSG

D o you sometimes feel swamped by your possessions? Do you seem to be spending more and more time keeping track of the things you own while making mental notes of the things you intend to buy? If so, here's a word of warning: your fondness for material possessions is getting in the way of your relationships—your relationships with the people around you and your relationship with God.

Society teaches us to honor possessions . . . God teaches us to honor people. And if we seek to be worthy followers of Christ, we must never invest too much energy in the acquisition of "stuff." Earthly riches are here today and all too soon gone. Our real riches, of course, are in heaven, and that's where we should focus our thoughts and our energy.

The more we stuff ourselves with material pleasures, the less we seem to appreciate life.

Barbara Johnson

Outside appearances, things like the clothes you wear or the car you drive, are important to other people but totally unimportant to God. Trust God.

Marie T. Freeman

As faithful stewards of what we have, ought we not to give earnest thought to our staggering surplus?

Elisabeth Elliot

It's sobering to contemplate how much time, effort, sacrifice, compromise, and attention we give to acquiring and increasing our supply of something that is totally insignificant in eternity.

Anne Graham Lotz

We are made spiritually lethargic by a steady diet of materialism.

Mary Morrison Suggs

Greed is enslaving. The more you have, the more you want—until eventually avarice consumes you.

Kay Arthur

And He told them, "Watch out and be on guard against all greed, because one's life is not in the abundance of his possessions."

Luke 12:15 HCSB

He who trusts in his riches will fall, but the righteous will flourish . . . .

Proverbs 11:28 NKJV

No one can serve two masters. The person will hate one master and love the other, or will follow one master and refuse to follow the other. You cannot serve both God and worldly riches.

Matthew 6:24 NCV

For the mind-set of the flesh is death, but the mind-set of the Spirit is life and peace.

Romans 8:6 HCSB

TODAY'S PRAYER OF GRACE

Dear Lord, keep me mindful that material possessions cannot bring me joy—my joy comes from You. I praise You, Father for Your gifts. Let me feel Your presence and share Your love with family, with friends, and with neighbors, this day and every day. Amen

THE IMPORTANCE OF DISCIPLINE

I discipline my body and bring it under strict control,
so that after preaching to others,
I myself will not be disqualified.
1 Corinthians 9:27 HCSB

God's Word is clear: as believers, we are called to lead lives of discipline, diligence, moderation, and maturity. But the world often tempts us to behave otherwise. Everywhere we turn, or so it seems, we are faced with powerful temptations to behave in undisciplined, ungodly ways.

We live in a world in which leisure is glorified and misbehavior is glamorized. But God has other plans. He did not create us for lives of mischief or mediocrity; He created us for far greater things.

Life's greatest rewards seldom fall into our laps; to the contrary, God rewards diligence and righteousness just as certainly as He punishes laziness and sin. As believers in a just God, we should behave accordingly.

I believe the reason so many are failing today is that they have not disciplined themselves to read God's Word consistently, day in and day out, and to apply it to every situation in life.

Kay Arthur

If I could just hang in there, being faithful to my own tasks, God would make me joyful and content. The responsibility is mine, but the power is His.

Peg Rankin

God "longs to be gracious" to us (Isaiah 30:18), and He carries out His judgment against our sin with holy sorrow, intending His discipline to be a vehicle of mercy toward us.

Nancy Groom

Real freedom means to welcome the responsibility it brings, to welcome the God-control it requires, to welcome the discipline that results, to welcome the maturity it creates.

Eugenia Price

The balance of affirmation and discipline, freedom and restraint, encouragement and warning is different for each child and season and generation, yet the absolutes of God's Word are necessary and trustworthy no matter how mercuric the time.

Gloria Gaither

He who heeds discipline shows the way to life, but whoever ignores correction leads others astray.

Proverbs 10:17 NIV

Folly is loud; she is undisciplined and without knowledge.

Proverbs 9:13 NIV

Whoever gives heed to instruction prospers, and blessed is he that trusts in the Lord.

Proverbs 16:20 NIV

My son, do not despise the chastening of the Lord, nor be discouraged when you are rebuked by Him.

Hebrews 12:5 NKJV

Today's Prayer of Grace

Heavenly Father, You are my rock and my protector, and I praise You. Make me a woman who understands the need to live a disciplined life. Let me teach others by the faithfulness of my conduct, and let me follow Your will and Your Word, today and every day. Amen

BEYOND DISCOURAGEMENT

*He gives power to the weak, and to those who have
no might He increases strength.*

Isaiah 40:29 NKJV

We Christians have many reasons to celebrate. God is in His heaven; Christ has risen, and we are the sheep of His flock. Yet sometimes, even the most devout believers may become discouraged. After all, we live in a world where expectations can be high and demands can be even higher.

When we fail to meet the expectations of others (or, for that matter, the expectations that we have for ourselves), we may be tempted to abandon hope. But God has other plans. He knows exactly how He intends to use us. Our task is to remain faithful until He does.

If you're a woman who has become discouraged with the direction of your day or your life, turn your thoughts and prayers to God. He is a God of possibility, not negativity. He will help you count your blessings instead of your hardships. And then, with a renewed spirit of optimism and hope, you can properly thank your Father in heaven for His blessings, for His love, and for His Son.

When we reach the end of our strength, wisdom, and personal resources, we enter into the beginning of his glorious provisions.

Patsy Clairmont

Overcoming discouragement is simply a matter of taking away the DIS and adding the EN.

Barbara Johnson

Working in the vineyard, / Working all the day, / Never be discouraged, / Only watch and pray.

Fanny Crosby

Just as courage is faith in good, so discouragement is faith in evil, and, while courage opens the door to good, discouragement opens it to evil.

Hannah Whitall Smith

The strength that we claim from God's Word does not depend on circumstances. Circumstances will be difficult, but our strength will be sufficient.

Corrie ten Boom

When we spend time with Christ, He supplies us with strength and encourages us in the pursuit of His ways.

Elizabeth George

But as for you, be strong; don't be discouraged, for your work has a reward.

2 Chronicles 15:7 HCSB

The Lord is the One who will go before you. He will be with you; He will not leave you or forsake you. Do not be afraid or discouraged.

Deuteronomy 31:8 HCSB

TODAY'S PRAYER OF GRACE

Dear Lord, when I am discouraged, give me perspective and faith. When I am weak, give me strength. When I am fearful, give me courage for the day ahead. I will trust in Your promises, Father, and I will live with the assurance that You are with me not only for this day, but also throughout all eternity. Amen

Day 25

Beyond Doubt

*Immediately the father of the child cried out and said
with tears, "Lord, I believe; help my unbelief!"*
Mark 9:24 NKJV

If you've never had any doubts about your faith, then
you can stop reading this page now and skip to the
next chapter. But if you've ever been plagued by
doubts about your faith or your God, keep reading.

Even some of the most faithful Christians are, at
times, beset by occasional bouts of discouragement and
doubt. But even when we feel far removed from God,
God is never far removed from us. He is always with us,
always willing to calm the storms of life—always willing to
replace our doubts with comfort and assurance.

Whenever you're plagued by doubts, that's precisely
the moment you should seek God's presence by genuinely
seeking to establish a deeper, more meaningful relationship with His Son. Then you may rest assured that in time,
God will calm your fears, answer your prayers, and restore
your confidence.

To wrestle with God does not mean that we have lost faith, but that we are fighting for it.

Sheila Walsh

Just as I am, though tossed about / With many a conflict, many a doubt, / Fightings and fears within, without, / O Lamb of God, I come, I come.

Charlotte Elliott

A life lived in God is not lived on the plane of feelings, but of the will.

Elisabeth Elliot

We are most vulnerable to the piercing winds of doubt when we distance ourselves from the mission and fellowship to which Christ has called us.

Joni Eareckson Tada

Disobedience to His Word will cause you to doubt.

Anne Graham Lotz

Fear and doubt are conquered by a faith that rejoices. And faith can rejoice because the promises of God are as certain as God Himself.

Kay Arthur

If you don't know what you're doing, pray to the Father. He loves to help. You'll get his help, and won't be condescended to when you ask for it. Ask boldly, believingly, without a second thought. People who "worry their prayers" are like wind-whipped waves. Don't think you're going to get anything from the Master that way, adrift at sea, keeping all your options open.

James 1:5-8 MSG

Purify your hearts, ye double-minded.

James 4:8 KJV

When doubts filled my mind, your comfort gave me renewed hope and cheer.

Psalm 94:19 NLT

TODAY'S PRAYER OF GRACE

Dear God, sometimes this world can be a puzzling place, filled with uncertainty and doubt. When I am unsure of my next step, keep me mindful that You are always near and that You can overcome any challenge. Give me faith, Father, and let me remember always that with Your love and Your power, I can live courageously and faithfully today and every day. Amen

A SPIRITUAL SICKNESS

All bitterness, anger and wrath, insult and slander must be
removed from you, along with all wickedness.
And be kind and compassionate to one another,
forgiving one another, just as God also forgave you in Christ.
Ephesians 4:31-32 HCSB

A re you a woman who is mired in the quicksand of bitterness or regret? If so, you are not only disobeying God's Word, you are also wasting your time. The world holds few if any rewards for those who remain angrily focused upon the past. Still, the act of forgiveness is difficult for all but the most saintly men and women.

Being frail, fallible, imperfect human beings, most of us are quick to anger, quick to blame, slow to forgive, and even slower to forget. Yet as Christians, we are commanded to forgive others, just as we, too, have been forgiven.

If there exists even one person—alive or dead—against whom you hold bitter feelings, it's time to forgive. Or, if you are embittered against yourself for some past mistake or shortcoming, it's finally time to forgive yourself and move on. Hatred, bitterness, and regret are not part of God's plan for your life. Forgiveness is.

Forgiveness is the key which unlocks
the door of resentment
and the handcuffs of hatred.
It breaks the chains of bitterness
and the shackles of selfishness.

—

Corrie ten Boom

Grudges are like hand grenades; it is wise to release them before they destroy you.

Barbara Johnson

Sin is any deed or memory that hampers or binds human personality.

Catherine Marshall

Forgiveness enables you to bury your grudge in icy earth. To put the past behind you. To flush resentment away by being the first to forgive. Forgiveness fashions your future. It is a brave and brash thing to do.

Barbara Johnson

You cannot live with a chip on your shoulder. Chips make you bend your body to balance them. And when you bend, you lose your poise, your balance, and the chip gets into you. The real you. You get hard.

Marita Bonner

Bitterness is a spiritual cancer, a rapidly growing malignancy that can consume your life. Bitterness cannot be ignored but must be healed at the very core, and only Christ can heal bitterness.

Beth Moore

Get rid of all bitterness, rage, anger, harsh words, and slander, as well as all types of malicious behavior. Instead, be kind to each other, tenderhearted, forgiving one another, just as God through Christ has forgiven you.

Ephesians 4:31–32 NLT

But now you must also put away all the following: anger, wrath, malice, slander, and filthy language from your mouth.

Colossians 3:8 HCSB

When you are angry, do not sin, and be sure to stop being angry before the end of the day. Do not give the devil a way to defeat you.

Ephesians 4:26–27 NCV

Today's Prayer of Grace

Dear Lord, free me from the poison of bitterness and the futility of blame. When I am bitter, I cannot sense Your presence; when I blame others, I cannot sense Your peace. Let me turn away from destructive emotions so that I may know the perfect peace and spiritual abundance that can be mine through Your Son, and when I discover His peace, let me share it with praise on my lips and love in my heart. Amen

DAY 27

YOUR OWN WORST CRITIC?

A devout life does bring wealth,
but it's the rich simplicity of being yourself before God.
1 Timothy 6:6 MSG

Are you your own worst critic? If so, it's time to become a little more understanding of the woman you see whenever you look into the mirror.

Millions of words have been written about various ways to improve self-image and increase self-esteem. Yet, maintaining a healthy self-image is, to a surprising extent, a matter of doing three things: 1. behaving ourselves 2. thinking healthy thoughts 3. finding a purpose for your life that pleases your Creator and yourself.

The Bible affirms the importance of self-acceptance by teaching Christians to love others as they love themselves (Matthew 22:37-40). God accepts us just as we are. And, if He accepts us—faults and all—then who are we to believe otherwise?

One of Satan's most effective ploys is to make us believe that we are small, insignificant, and worthless.

Susan Lenzkes

Give yourself a gift today: be present with yourself. God is. Enjoy your own personality. God does.

Barbara Johnson

I may have tasted peace, but to believe that the God of heaven and earth calls me beautiful—well, I think I could rest in that. If I truly knew that He was smitten with me, maybe I could take a deep breath, square my shoulders, and go out to face the world with confidence.

Angela Thomas

Being loved by Him whose opinion matters most gives us the security to risk loving, too—even loving ourselves.

Gloria Gaither

Christian women are often blocked from maximizing their potential because they do not understand the power of the Holy Spirit within them. Many Christian women struggle with the I'm-not-good-enough-smart-enough-talented-enough syndrome. A leader of women understands that every daughter of the King has been uniquely designed and equipped for a purpose.

Susan Hunt

Finally, brethren, whatever things are true, whatever things are noble, whatever things are just, whatever things are pure, whatever things are lovely, whatever things are of good report, if there is any virtue and if there is anything praiseworthy— meditate on these things.

—

Philippians 4:8 NKJV

For You have made him a little lower than the angels, and You have crowned him with glory and honor.

Psalm 8:5 NKJV

How happy are those whose way is blameless, who live according to the law of the Lord! Happy are those who keep His decrees and seek Him with all their heart.

Psalm 119:1-2 HCSB

Happy is the one whose help is the God of Jacob, whose hope is in the Lord his God.

Psalm 146:5 HCSB

If God is for us, who is against us?

Romans 8:31 HCSB

Today's Prayer of Grace

Lord, I have so much to learn and so many ways to improve myself, but You love me just as I am. Thank You for Your love and for Your Son. And, help me to become the person that You want me to become. Amen

Day 28

Praising God for His Abundance

I came that they may have life, and have it abundantly.
John 10:10 NASB

God's gifts are available to all, but they are not guaranteed; those gifts must be claimed by those who choose to follow Christ. As believers, we are free to accept God's gifts, or not; that choice, and the consequences that result from it, are ours and ours alone.

The 10th chapter of John tells us that Christ came to earth so that our lives might be filled with abundance. But what, exactly, did Jesus mean when He promised "life . . . more abundantly"? Was Jesus referring to material possessions or financial wealth? Hardly. When Jesus declared Himself the shepherd of mankind (John 10:7-9), He offered a different kind of abundance: a spiritual richness that extends beyond the temporal boundaries of this world.

If you are a thoughtful believer, you will open yourself to Christ's spiritual abundance by following Him completely and without reservation. When you do, you will receive the love, the peace, and the joy that He has promised.

The fullness of life in Christ is available to all who seek it and claim it. Count yourself among that number. Seek first the salvation that is available through a personal relationship with Jesus, and then claim the abundance that can—and should—be yours.

Do you sincerely seek the riches that our Savior offers to those who give themselves to Him? Then follow Him—and receive the blessings that He has promised. When you establish an intimate, passionate relationship with Christ, you are then free to claim the love, the protection, and the spiritual abundance that the Shepherd offers His sheep.

Get ready for God to show you
not only His pleasure, but His approval.

—

Joni Eareckson Tada

God is the giver, and we are the receivers. And His richest gifts are bestowed not upon those who do the greatest things, but upon those who accept His abundance and His grace.

Hannah Whitall Smith

God has promised us abundance, peace, and eternal life. These treasures are ours for the asking; all we must do is claim them. One of the great mysteries of life is why on earth do so many of us wait so very long to lay claim to God's gifts?

Marie T. Freeman

Yes, we were created for His holy pleasure, but we will ultimately—if not immediately—find much pleasure in His pleasure.

Beth Moore

It would be wrong to have a "poverty complex," for to think ourselves paupers is to deny either the King's riches or to deny our being His children.

Catherine Marshall

Jesus intended for us to be overwhelmed by the blessings of regular days. He said it was the reason he had come: "I am come that they might have life, and that they might have it more abundantly."

Gloria Gaither

Live in me. Make your home in me just as I do in you. In the same way that a branch can't bear grapes by itself but only by being joined to the vine, you can't bear fruit unless you are joined with me. I am the Vine, you are the branches. When you're joined with me and I with you, the relation intimate and organic, the harvest is sure to be abundant.

John 15:4-5 MSG

Until now you have asked for nothing in My name. Ask and you will receive, that your joy may be complete.

John 16:24 HCSB

The master was full of praise. "Well done, my good and faithful servant. You have been faithful in handling this small amount, so now I will give you many more responsibilities. Let's celebrate together!"

Matthew 25:21 NLT

TODAY'S PRAYER OF GRACE

I praise You, Lord, for the abundant life given through Your Son Jesus Christ. You have blessed me beyond measure. Make me a faithful steward of the gifts You have given me so that I may share Your abundance with all who cross my path. Amen

DAY 29

THE NEED FOR SILENCE

Be silent before the Lord and wait expectantly for Him.
Psalm 37:7 HCSB

The world seems to grow louder day by day, and our senses seem to be invaded at every turn. If we allow the distractions of a clamorous society to separate us from God's peace, we do ourselves a profound disservice. Our task, as dutiful believers, is to carve out moments of silence in a world filled with noise.

If we are to maintain righteous minds and comp-assionate hearts, we must take time each day for prayer and for meditation. We must make ourselves still in the presence of our Creator. We must quiet our minds and our hearts so that we might sense God's will and His love.

Has the hectic pace of life robbed you of God's peace? If so, it's time to reorder your priorities and your life. Nothing is more important than the time you spend with your Heavenly Father. So be still and claim the genuine peace that is found in the silent moments you spend with God.

If you, too, will learn to wait upon God, to get alone with Him, and remain silent so that you can hear His voice when He is ready to speak to you, what a difference it will make in your life!

Kay Arthur

Because Jesus Christ is our Great High Priest, not only can we approach God without a human "go-between," we can also hear and learn from God in some sacred moments without one.

Beth Moore

Deepest communion with God is beyond words, on the other side of silence.

Madeleine L'Engle

The world is full of noise. Might we not set ourselves to learn silence, stillness, solitude?

Elisabeth Elliot

Be still, and in the quiet moments, listen to the voice of your Heavenly Father. His words can renew your spirit. No one knows you and your needs like He does.

Janet L. Weaver

I always begin my prayers
in silence, for it is in the silence of
the heart that God speaks.

—

Mother Teresa

In quietness and trust is your strength.

Isaiah 30:15 NASB

Be still, and know that I am God.

Psalm 46:10 NKJV

I wait quietly before God, for my salvation comes from him.

Psalm 62:1 NLT

My soul, wait silently for God alone, for my expectation is from Him.

Psalm 62:5 NKJV

TODAY'S PRAYER OF GRACE

Dear Lord, in the quiet moments of this day, I will turn my thoughts and prayers to You. In silence I will sense Your presence, and I will seek Your will for my life, knowing that when I accept Your peace, I will be blessed today and throughout eternity. Amen

Day 30

Today's Theme: Speech

Being Careful with Your Words

Careful words make for a careful life;
careless talk may ruin everything.

Proverbs 13:3 MSG

How important are the words we speak? More important than we may realize. Our words have echoes that extend beyond place or time. If our words are encouraging, we can lift others up; if our words are hurtful, we can hold others back.

Jesus said, "In everything, do to others what you would have them do to you, for this sums up the Law and the Prophets" (Matthew 7:12 NIV). This commandment is, indeed, the Golden Rule for Christians of every generation. And if we are to observe the Golden Rule, we must be careful to speak words of encouragement, hope, and truth to all those who cross our paths.

Do you seek to be a source of encouragement to others? And, do you seek to be a worthy ambassador for Christ? If so, you must speak words that are worthy of your

Savior. So avoid angry outbursts. Refrain from impulsive outpourings. Terminate tantrums. Instead, speak words of encouragement and hope to your family and friends, who, by the way, need all the hope and encouragement they can find.

A little kindly advice is better than a great deal of scolding.

Fanny Crosby

When you talk, choose the very same words that you would use if Jesus were looking over your shoulder. Because He is.

Marie T. Freeman

It is time that the followers of Jesus revise their language and learn to speak respectfully of non-Christian peoples.

Lottie Moon

The battle of the tongue is won not in the mouth, but in the heart.

Annie Chapman

Pleasant words are a honeycomb: sweet to the taste and health to the body.

Proverbs 16:24 HCSB

For the one who wants to love life and to see good days must keep his tongue from evil and his lips from speaking deceit.

1 Peter 3:10 HCSB

Avoid irreverent, empty speech, for this will produce an even greater measure of godlessness.

2 Timothy 2:16 HCSB

No rotten talk should come from your mouth, but only what is good for the building up of someone in need, in order to give grace to those who hear.

Ephesians 4:29 HCSB

TODAY'S PRAYER OF GRACE

Lord, You have warned me that I will be judged by the words I speak. And, You have commanded me to choose my words carefully so that I might be a source of encouragement and hope to all whom I meet. Keep me mindful, Lord, that I have influence on many people . . . make me an influence for good. And may the words that I speak today be worthy of the One who has saved me forever. Amen

Praise Him

And those who have reason to be thankful should
continually sing praises to the Lord.
James 5:13 NLT

Because we have been saved by God's only Son, we must never lose hope in the priceless gifts of eternal love and eternal life. And, because we are so richly blessed, we must approach our Heavenly Father with reverence and thanksgiving.

Sometimes, in our rush "to get things done," we simply don't stop long enough to pause and thank our Creator for the countless blessings He has bestowed upon us. But when we slow down and express our gratitude to the One who made us, we enrich our own lives and the lives of those around us.

Thanksgiving should become a habit, a regular part of our daily routines. God has blessed us beyond measure, and we owe Him everything, including our eternal praise. Let us praise Him today, tomorrow, and throughout eternity.

Our God is the sovereign Creator of the universe! He loves us as His own children and has provided every good thing we have; He is worthy of our praise every moment.

Shirley Dobson

Preoccupy my thoughts with your praise beginning today.

Joni Eareckson Tada

Two wings are necessary to lift our souls toward God: prayer and praise. Prayer asks. Praise accepts the answer.

Mrs. Charles E. Cowman

Words fail to express my love for this holy Book, my gratitude for its author, for His love and goodness. How shall I thank him for it?

Lottie Moon

This is my story, this is my song, praising my Savior, all the day long.

Fanny Crosby

Nothing we do is more powerful or more life-changing than praising God.

Stormie Omartian

Praise the Lord, all nations! Glorify Him, all peoples! For great is His faithful love to us; the Lord's faithfulness endures forever. Hallelujah!

Psalm 117 HCSB

But I will hope continually and will praise You more and more.

Psalm 71:14 HCSB

Therefore, through Him let us continually offer up to God a sacrifice of praise, that is, the fruit of our lips that confess His name.

Hebrews 13:15 HCSB

So that at the name of Jesus every knee should bow—of those who are in heaven and on earth and under the earth—and every tongue should confess that Jesus Christ is Lord, to the glory of God the Father.

Philippians 2:10-11 HCSB

Today's Prayer of Grace

Dear Lord, today and every day I will praise You. I come to You with hope in my heart and words of thanksgiving on my lips. Let me follow in Christ's footsteps, and let my thoughts, my prayers, my words, and my deeds honor You now and forever. Amen

GOD'S CALLING

I, therefore, the prisoner in the Lord, urge you to walk worthy of the calling you have received.

Ephesians 4:1 HCSB

It is terribly important that you heed God's calling by discovering and developing your talents and your spiritual gifts. If you seek to make a difference—and if you seek to bear eternal fruit—you must discover your gifts and begin using them for the glory of God.

Every believer has at least one gift. In John 15:16, Jesus says, "You did not choose Me, but I chose you and appointed you that you should go and bear fruit, and that your fruit should remain, that whatever you ask the Father in My name He may give you." Have you found your special calling? If not, keep searching and keep praying until you find it. God has important work for you to do, and the time to begin that work is now.

If God has called you, do not spend time looking over your shoulder to see who is following you.

Corrie ten Boom

If God's Word, your circumstances, and the counsel of others line up, and if you sense his provision, I'd say go for it.

Luci Swindoll

The things that we feel most deeply we ought to learn to be silent about, at least until we have talked them over thoroughly with God.

Elisabeth Elliot

From the very moment one feels called to act is born the strength to bear whatever horror one will feel or see. In some inexplicable way, terror loses its overwhelming power when it becomes a task that must be faced.

Emmi Bonhoeffer

I may have tasted peace, but to believe that the God of heaven and earth calls me beautiful—well, I think I could rest in that. If I truly knew that He was smitten with me, maybe I could take a deep breath, square my shoulders, and go out to face the world with confidence.

Angela Thomas

God calls us to seek Him daily
in order to serve Him daily.

—

Sheila Cragg

But as God has distributed to each one, as the Lord has called each one, so let him walk.

1 Corinthians 7:17 NKJV

I pray that the eyes of your heart may be enlightened so you may know what is the hope of His calling, what are the glorious riches of His inheritance among the saints, and what is the immeasurable greatness of His power to us who believe, according to the working of His vast strength.

Ephesians 1:18-19 HCSB

One thing I do, forgetting those things which are behind and reaching forward to those things which are ahead, I press toward the goal for the prize of the upward call of God in Christ Jesus.

Philippians 3:13-14 NKJV

So the last shall be first, and the first last: for many be called, but few chosen.

Matthew 20:16 KJV

Today's Prayer of Grace

Heavenly Father, You have called me, and I acknowledge that calling. In these quiet moments before this busy day unfolds, I come to You. I will study Your Word and seek Your guidance. Give me the wisdom to know Your will for my life and the courage to follow wherever You may lead me, today and forever. Amen

MAKING TIME FOR GOD

Don't burn out; keep yourselves fueled and aflame.
Be alert servants of the Master, cheerfully expectant.
Don't quit in hard times; pray all the harder.

Romans 12:11-12 MSG

Has the busy pace of life robbed you of the peace that might otherwise be yours through Jesus Christ? If so, you are simply too busy for your own good. Through His Son Jesus, God offers you a peace that passes human understanding, but He won't force His peace upon you; in order to experience it, you must slow down long enough to sense His presence and His love.

Each waking moment holds the potential to think a creative thought or offer a heartfelt prayer. So even if you're a woman with too many demands and too few hours in which to meet them, don't panic. Instead, be comforted in the knowledge that when you sincerely seek to discover God's purpose for your life, He will respond in marvelous and surprising ways. Remember: this is the day that He has made and that He has filled it with countless opportunities to love, to serve, and to seek His guidance. Seize those opportunities today, and keep seizing them every day that you live.

When a church member gets overactive and public worship is neglected, his or her relationship with God will be damaged.

Anne Ortlund

Getting things accomplished isn't nearly as important as taking time for love.

Janette Oke

Life is not intended to be simply a round of work, no matter how interesting and important that work may be. A moment's pause to watch the glory of a sunrise or a sunset is soul satisfying, while a bird's song will set the steps to music all day long.

Laura Ingalls Wilder

The demand of every day kept me so busy that I subconsciously equated my busyness with commitment to Christ.

Vonette Bright

Careful planning puts you ahead in the long run; hurry and scurry puts you further behind.

Proverbs 21:5 MSG

You can't go wrong when you love others. When you add up everything in the law code, the sum total is love. But make sure that you don't get so absorbed and exhausted in taking care of all your day-by-day obligations that you lose track of the time and doze off, oblivious to God.

Romans 13:10-11 MSG

Jesus said, "You're tied down to the mundane; I'm in touch with what is beyond your horizons. You live in terms of what you see and touch. I'm living on other terms. I told you that you were missing God in all this. You're at a dead end. If you won't believe I am who I say I am, you're at the dead end of sins. You're missing God in your lives."

John 8:23-24 MSG

Today's Prayer of Grace

Dear Lord, You are my rock, and I praise You for Your blessings. But sometimes, I am distracted by the busyness of the day or the demands of the moment. When I am worried or anxious, Father, turn my thoughts back to You. Help me to trust Your will, to follow Your commands, and to accept Your peace, today and forever. Amen

GOD'S LOVE

This is how much God loved the world: He gave his Son,
his one and only Son. And this is why:
so that no one need be destroyed; by believing in him
anyone can have a whole and lasting life.

John 3:16 MSG

God's love for you is deeper and more profound than you can fathom. And now, precisely because you are a wondrous creation treasured by God, a question presents itself: What will you do in response to God's love? Will you ignore it or embrace it? Will you return it or neglect it? The decision, of course, is yours and yours alone.

When you embrace God's love, you are forever changed. When you embrace God's love, you feel differently about yourself, your neighbors, and your world. When you embrace God's love, you share His message and you obey His commandments.

When you accept the Father's grace and share the His love, you are blessed here on earth and throughout all eternity. Accept His love today.

A major turning point in my life came when I realized that being able to trust God is grounded in staking the whole of my being on the reality that he loves me.

Paula Rinehart

Being loved by Him whose opinion matters most gives us the security to risk loving, too—even loving ourselves.

Gloria Gaither

When you invite the love of God into your heart, everything in the world looks different, including you.

Marie T. Freeman

We are of such value to God that He came to live among us . . . and to guide us home. He will go to any length to seek us, even to being lifted high upon the cross to draw us back to Himself. We can only respond by loving God for His love.

Catherine of Siena

We must mirror God's love in the midst of a world full of hatred. We are the mirrors of God's love, so we may show Jesus by our lives.

Corrie ten Boom

God loves us enough
to make us ultimately miserable
in our rebellion.

———

Beth Moore

Whoever is wise will observe these things, and they will understand the lovingkindness of the Lord.

Psalm 107:43 NKJV

Unfailing love surrounds those who trust the LORD.

Psalm 32:10 NLT

Help me, Lord my God; save me according to Your faithful love.

Psalm 109:26 HCSB

The Lord is gracious and compassionate, slow to anger and great in faithful love. The Lord is good to everyone; His compassion [rests] on all He has made.

Psalm 145:8-9 HCSB

TODAY'S PRAYER OF GRACE

Thank You, Lord, for Your love. Your love is boundless, infinite, and eternal. Today, let me pause and reflect upon Your love for me, and let me share that love with all those who cross my path. Amen

Day 35

TRUSTING GOD'S WISDOM

*Happy is the person who finds wisdom
and gains understanding.*

Proverbs 3:13 NLT

Sometimes, amid the concerns of everyday life, we lose perspective. Life seems out of balance as we confront an array of demands that sap our strength and cloud our thoughts. What's needed is a renewed faith, a fresh perspective, and God's wisdom.

Here in the 21st century, commentary is commonplace and information is everywhere. But the ultimate source of wisdom, the kind of timeless wisdom that God willingly shares with His children, is still available from a single unique source: the Holy Bible.

The wisdom of the world changes with the ever-shifting sands of public opinion. God's wisdom does not. His wisdom is eternal. It never changes. And it most certainly is the wisdom that you must use to plan your day, your life, and your eternal destiny.

This is my song through endless ages: Jesus led me all the way.

Fanny Crosby

Wisdom is knowledge applied. Head knowledge is useless on the battlefield. Knowledge stamped on the heart makes one wise.

Beth Moore

When you and I are related to Jesus Christ, our strength and wisdom and peace and joy and love and hope may run out, but His life rushes in to keep us filled to the brim. We are showered with blessings, not because of anything we have or have not done, but simply because of Him.

Anne Graham Lotz

If we neglect the Bible, we cannot expect to benefit from the wisdom and direction that result from knowing God's Word.

Vonette Bright

Knowledge can be found in books or in school. Wisdom, on the other hand, starts with God . . . and ends there.

Marie T. Freeman

He teaches us, not just to
let us see ourselves correctly,
but to help us see Him correctly.

—

Kathy Troccoli

The fear of the Lord is the beginning of wisdom; a good understanding have all those who do His commandments. His praise endures forever.

Psalm 111:10 NKJV

So teach us to number our days, that we may gain a heart of wisdom.

Psalm 90:12 NKJV

Teach me, O Lord, the way of Your statutes, and I shall keep it to the end.

Psalm 119:33 NKJV

A wise man will hear and increase learning, and a man of understanding will attain wise counsel.

Proverbs 1:5 NKJV

Today's Prayer of Grace

Dear Lord, when I trust in the wisdom of the world, I am often led astray, but when I trust in Your wisdom, I build my life upon a firm foundation. Today and every day I will trust Your Word and follow it, knowing that the ultimate wisdom is Your wisdom and the ultimate truth is Your truth. Amen

TRUST HIS PERFECT PLAN

You will show me the path of life;
in Your presence is fullness of joy;
at Your right hand are pleasures forevermore.
Psalm 16:11 NKJV

God has a plan for your life. He understands that plan as thoroughly and completely as He knows you. And, if you seek God's will earnestly and prayerfully, He will make His plans known to you in His own time and in His own way.

If you sincerely seek to live in accordance with God's will for your life, you will live in accordance with His commandments. You will study God's Word, and you will be watchful for His signs.

Sometimes, God's plans seem unmistakably clear to you. But other times, He may lead you through the wilderness before He directs you to the Promised Land. So be patient and keep seeking His will for your life. When you do, you'll be amazed at the marvelous things that an all-powerful, all-knowing God can do.

God in Christ is the author and finisher of my faith. He knows exactly what needs to happen in my life for my faith to grow. He designs the perfect program for me.

Mary Morrison Suggs

When the dream of our heart is one that God has planted there, a strange happiness flows into us. At that moment, all of the spiritual resources of the universe are released to help us. Our praying is then at one with the will of God and becomes a channel for the Creator's purposes for us and our world.

Catherine Marshall

God has plans—not problems—for our lives. Before she died in the concentration camp in Ravensbruck, my sister Betsie said to me, "Corrie, your whole life has been a training for the work you are doing here in prison—and for the work you will do afterward."

Corrie ten Boom

God has His reasons. He has His purposes. Ours is an intentional God, brimming over with motive and mission. He never does things capriciously or decides with the flip of a coin.

Joni Eareckson Tada

God prepared a plan
for your life alone—
and neither man nor the devil
can destroy that plan.

—

Kay Arthur

"I say this because I know what I am planning for you," says the Lord. *"I have good plans for you, not plans to hurt you. I will give you hope and a good future."*

Jeremiah 29:11 NCV

People may make plans in their minds, but the Lord decides what they will do.

Proverbs 16:9 NCV

There is no wisdom, no insight, no plan that can succeed against the Lord.

Proverbs 21:30 NIV

Unless the Lord builds a house, the work of the builders is useless.

Psalm 127:1 NLT

TODAY'S PRAYER OF GRACE

Lord, You have a plan for my life that is grander than I can imagine. Let Your purposes be my purposes. Let Your will be my will. When I am confused, give me clarity. When I am frightened, give me courage. Let me be Your faithful servant, always seeking Your guidance for my life. And, let me always be a shining beacon for Your Son today and every day that I live. Amen

INTEGRITY ALWAYS

The godly walk with integrity;
blessed are their children after them.
Proverbs 20:7 NLT

Wise women understand that integrity is a crucial building block in the foundation of a well-lived life. Integrity is built slowly over a lifetime. It is the sum of every right decision, every honest word, every noble thought, and every heartfelt prayer. It is forged on the anvil of honorable work and polished by the twin virtues of generosity and humility. Integrity is a precious thing—difficult to build, but easy to tear down; godly women value it and protect it at all costs.

As believers in Christ, we must seek to live each day with discipline, honesty, and faith. When we do, at least two things happen: integrity becomes a habit, and God blesses us because of our obedience to Him.

Living a life of integrity isn't always the easiest way, but it is always the right way. And God clearly intends that it should be our way, too.

God never called us to naïveté. He called us to integrity…. The biblical concept of integrity emphasizes mature innocence not childlike ignorance.

Beth Moore

The greatest honor you can give Almighty God is to live gladly and joyfully because of the knowledge of His love.

Juliana of Norwich

There is a transcendent power in example. We reform others unconsciously when we walk uprightly.

Anne Sophie Swetchine

Often, our character is at greater risk in prosperity than in adversity.

Beth Moore

If in the integrity of my heart I speak the words, Thy will be done, I must be willing, if the answer requires it, that my will be undone. It is a prayer of commitment and relinquishment.

Elisabeth Elliot

Character contributes to beauty. It fortifies a woman as her youth fades. A mode of conduct, a standard of courage, discipline, fortitude and integrity can do a great deal to make a woman beautiful.

Jacqueline Bisset

Till I die, I will not deny my integrity. I will maintain my righteousness and never let go of it; my conscience will not reproach me as long as I live.

Job 27:5-6 NIV

May integrity and uprightness protect me, because my hope is in you.

Psalm 25:21 NIV

In everything set them an example by doing what is good. In your teaching show integrity, seriousness and soundness of speech that cannot be condemned, so that those who oppose you may be ashamed because they have nothing bad to say about us.

Titus 2:7 NIV

A good name is to be chosen rather than great riches, loving favor rather than silver and gold.

Proverbs 22:1 NKJV

TODAY'S PRAYER OF GRACE

Dear Lord, You search my heart and know me far better than I know myself. May I be Your worthy servant, and may I live according to Your commandments. Let me be a woman of integrity, Lord, and let my words and deeds be a testimony to You, today and always. Amen

DAY 38

LOOKING FOR MIRACLES

With God's power working in us, God can do much,
much more than anything we can ask or imagine.
Ephesians 3:20 NCV

Do you believe in an all-powerful God who can do miraculous things in you and through you? You should. But perhaps, as you have faced the inevitable struggles of life-here-on-earth, you have—without realizing it—placed limitations on God. To do so is a profound mistake. God's power has no such limitations, and He can work mighty miracles in your own life if you let Him.

Do you lack a firm faith in God's power to perform miracles for you and your loved ones? If so, you are attempting to place limitations on a God who has none. Instead of doubting your Heavenly Father, you must place yourself in His hands. Instead of doubting God's power, you must trust it. Expect Him to work miracles, and be watchful. With God, absolutely nothing is impossible, including an amazing assortment of miracles that He stands ready, willing, and perfectly able to perform for you and yours.

God's faithfulness and grace make the impossible possible.

Sheila Walsh

Faith means believing in realities that go beyond sense and sight. It is the awareness of unseen divine realities all around you.

Joni Eareckson Tada

I could go through this day oblivious to the miracles all around me or I could tune in and "enjoy."

Gloria Gaither

To be a Christian is to believe in the impossible. Jesus was God. Jesus was human.

Madeleine L'Engle

The most profane word we use is "hopeless." When you say a situation or person is hopeless, you are slamming the door in the face of God.

Kathy Troccoli

Are you looking for a miracle? If you keep your eyes wide open and trust in God, you won't have to look very far.

Marie T. Freeman

Looking at them, Jesus said, "With men it is impossible, but not with God, because all things are possible with God."

Mark 10:27 HCSB

I assure you: The one who believes in Me will also do the works that I do. And he will do even greater works than these, because I am going to the Father.

John 14:12 HCSB

But as it is written: "Eye has not seen, nor ear heard, nor have entered into the heart of man the things which God has prepared for those who love Him."

1 Corinthians 2:9 NKJV

For nothing will be impossible with God.

Luke 1:37 HCSB

Today's Prayer of Grace

Heavenly Father, Your infinite power is beyond human understanding. With You, Lord, nothing is impossible. Keep me always mindful of Your power, and let me share the glorious message of Your miracles. When I lose hope, give me faith; when others lose hope, let me tell them of Your glory and Your works. Today, Lord, let me expect the miraculous, let me praise You, and let me give thanks for Your miracles. Amen

Managing Change

One Lord, one faith, one baptism, one God and Father of all,
who is above all and through all and in all.

Ephesians 4:5-6 HCSB

O ur world is in a state of constant change. God is not. At times, the world seems to be trembling beneath our feet. But we can be comforted in the knowledge that our Heavenly Father is the rock that cannot be shaken. His Word promises, "I am the Lord, I do not change" (Malachi 3:6 NKJV).

Every day that we live, we mortals encounter a multitude of changes—some good, some not so good. And on occasion, all of us must endure life-changing personal losses that leave us breathless. When we do, our loving Heavenly Father stands ready to protect us, to comfort us, to guide us, and, in time, to heal us.

Are you facing difficult circumstances or unwelcome changes? If so, please remember that God is far bigger than any problem you may face. So, instead of worrying about life's inevitable challenges, put your faith in the Father and His only begotten Son: "Jesus Christ is the same yesterday, today, and forever" (Hebrews 13:8 HCSB). And rest assured: It is precisely because your Savior does not change that you can face your challenges with courage for this day and hope for the future.

We do not love each other without changing each other. We do not observe the world around us without in some way changing it, and being changed ourselves.

Madeleine L'Engle

The Holy Spirit can reveal to you why you are stuck, and he can empower you to change (although he won't usually do all the work without your involvement).

Patsy Clairmont

With God, it isn't who you were that matters; it's who you are becoming.

Liz Curtis Higgs

Let nothing disturb you, nothing frighten you; all things are passing; God never changes.

St. Teresa of Avila

The undeniable gospel is this: a transformed life.

Liz Curtis Higgs

John said, "Change your hearts and lives because the kingdom of heaven is near."

Matthew 3:2 NCV

Therefore do not worry about tomorrow, for tomorrow will worry about itself. Each day has enough trouble of its own.

Matthew 6:34 NIV

The sensible see danger and take cover; the foolish keep going and are punished.

Proverbs 27:12 HCSB

There is a time for everything, and a season for every activity under heaven.

Ecclesiastes 3:1 NIV

TODAY'S PRAYER OF GRACE

Dear Lord, our world is constantly changing. When I face the inevitable transitions of life, I will turn to You for strength and assurance. Thank You, Father, for love that is unchanging and everlasting. Amen

He Rewards Integrity

We also have joy with our troubles, because we know that these troubles produce patience. And patience produces character, and character produces hope.

Romans 5:3-4 NCV

Beth Moore correctly observed, "Those who walk in truth walk in liberty." Godly men and women agree. As believers in Christ, we must seek to live each day with discipline, honesty, and faith. When we do, at least two things happen: integrity becomes a habit, and God blesses us because of our obedience to Him. Living a life of integrity isn't always the easiest way, but it is always the right way . . . and God clearly intends that it should be our way, too.

Character isn't built overnight; it is built slowly over a lifetime. It is the sum of every sensible choice, every honorable decision, and every honest word. It is forged on the anvil of sincerity and polished by the virtue of fairness. Character is a precious thing—preserve yours at all costs.

So, the next time you're tempted to bend the truth—or to break it—ask yourself this simple question: "What does God want me to do?" Then listen carefully to your conscience. When you do, your actions will be honorable, and your character will take care of itself.

Often, our character is at greater risk
in prosperity than in adversity.

—

Beth Moore

Character isn't inherited. One builds it daily by the way one thinks and acts, thought by thought, action by action.

Helen Gahagan Douglas

There is something about having endured great loss that brings purity of purpose and strength of character.

Barbara Johnson

Character cannot be developed in ease and quiet. Only through experience of trial and suffering can the soul be strengthened, vision cleared, ambition inspired, and success achieved.

Helen Keller

Character builds slowly, but it can be torn down with incredible swiftness.

Faith Baldwin

Each one of us is God's special work of art. Through us, He teaches and inspires, delights and encourages, informs and uplifts all those who view our lives. God, the master artist, is most concerned about expressing Himself—His thoughts and His intentions—through what He paints in our characters.

Joni Eareckson Tada

As the water reflects the face, so the heart reflects the person.

Proverbs 27:19 HCSB

Blessed is the man who walks not in the counsel of the ungodly, nor stands in the path of sinners, nor sits in the seat of the scornful; but his delight is in the law of the Lord, and in His law he meditates day and night. He shall be like a tree planted by the rivers of water, that brings forth its fruit in its season, whose leaf also shall not wither; and whatever he does shall prosper.

Psalm 1:1-3 NKJV

A good name is to be chosen rather than great riches, loving favor rather than silver and gold.

Proverbs 22:1 NKJV

Do not be deceived: "Evil company corrupts good habits."

1 Corinthians 15:33 NKJV

TODAY'S PRAYER OF GRACE

Dear Lord, every day can be an exercise in character-building, and that's what I intend to make this day. I will be mindful that my thoughts and actions have great consequences, consequences in my own life and in the lives of my loved ones. I will strive to make my thoughts and actions pleasing to You, so that I may be an instrument of Your peace, today and every day. Amen

BEYOND TEMPTATION

Then Jesus told him, "Go away, Satan! For it is written:
You must worship the Lord your God,
and you must serve Him only."

Matthew 4:10 HCSB

After fasting forty days and nights in the desert, Jesus was tempted by Satan. Christ used Scripture to rebuke the devil (Matthew 4:1-11). We must do likewise. The Holy Bible provides us with a perfect blueprint for righteous living. If we consult that blueprint daily and follow it carefully, we build our lives according to God's plan.

We live in a world that is brimming with opportunities to stray from God's will. Ours is a society filled with temptations, a place where it is all too easy to disobey God. We, like our Savior, must guard ourselves against these temptations. We do so, in part, through prayer and through a careful reading of God's Word.

The battle against Satan is ongoing. Be vigilant, and call upon your Heavenly Father to protect you. When you petition Him with a sincere heart, God will be your shield, now and forever.

Temptation is not a sin. Even Jesus was tempted. The Lord Jesus gives you the strength needed to resist temptation.

Corrie ten Boom

The devil's most devilish when respectable.

Elizabeth Barrett Browning

In the Garden of Gethsemane, Jesus went through agony of soul in His efforts to resist the temptation to do what He felt like doing rather than what He knew was God's will for Him.

Joyce Meyer

We, as God's people, are not only to stay far away from sin and sinners who would entice us, but we are to be so like our God that we mourn over sin.

Kay Arthur

Do not fight the temptation in detail. Turn from it. Look ONLY at your Lord. Sing. Read. Work.

Amy Carmichael

Because Christ has faced our every temptation without sin, we never face a temptation that has no door of escape.

Beth Moore

No temptation has seized you except what is common to man. And God is faithful; he will not let you be tempted beyond what you can bear. But when you are tempted, he will also provide a way out so that you can stand up under it.

1 Corinthians 10:13 NIV

Be sober, be vigilant; because your adversary the devil walks about like a roaring lion, seeking whom he may devour.

1 Peter 5:8 NKJV

The Lord knows how to deliver the godly out of temptations.

2 Peter 2:9 NKJV

Put on the whole armor of God, that you may be able to stand against the wiles of the devil.

Ephesians 6:11 NKJV

Today's Prayer of Grace

Dear Lord, this world is filled with temptations, distractions, and frustrations. When I turn my thoughts away from You and Your Word, Lord, I suffer bitter consequences. But, when I trust in Your commandments, I am safe. Direct my path far from the temptations and distractions of the world. Let me discover Your will and follow it, Dear Lord, this day and always. Amen

BEYOND THE FRUSTRATIONS

When you are angry, do not sin,
and be sure to stop being angry before the end of the day.
Do not give the devil a way to defeat you.
Ephesians 4:26-27 NCV

Sometimes, anger is appropriate. Even Jesus became angry when confronted with the moneychangers in the temple. On occasion, you, like Jesus, will confront evil, and when you do, you may respond as He did: vigorously and without reservation. But, more often than not, your frustrations will be of the more mundane variety. As long as you live here on earth, you will face countless opportunities to lose your temper over small, relatively insignificant events: a traffic jam, a spilled cup of coffee, an inconsiderate comment, a broken promise. When you are tempted to lose your temper over the minor inconveniences of life, don't. Turn away from anger, hatred, bitterness, and regret. Turn instead to God.

Anger unresolved will only bring you woe.

Kay Arthur

There is no sin nor wrong that gives a man such a foretaste of hell in this life as anger and impatience.

St. Catherine of Siena

Is there somebody who's always getting your goat? Talk to the Shepherd.

Anonymous

Life is too short to spend it being angry, bored, or dull.

Barbara Johnson

When something robs you of your peace of mind, ask yourself if it is worth the energy you are expending on it. If not, then put it out of your mind in an act of discipline. Every time the thought of "it" returns, refuse it.

Kay Arthur

If your temper gets the best of you . . . then other people get to see the worst in you.

Marie T. Freeman

Don't let your spirit rush to be angry, for anger abides in the heart of fools.

Ecclesiastes 7:9 HCSB

My dearly loved brothers, understand this: everyone must be quick to hear, slow to speak, and slow to anger, for man's anger does not accomplish God's righteousness.

James 1:19-20 HCSB

A fool's displeasure is known at once, but whoever ignores an insult is sensible.

Proverbs 12:16 HCSB

But now you must also put away all the following: anger, wrath, malice, slander, and filthy language from your mouth.

Colossians 3:8 HCSB

Today's Prayer of Grace

Lord, sometimes, I am quick to anger and slow to forgive. But I know, Lord, that You seek abundance and peace for my life. Forgiveness is Your commandment; empower me to follow the example of Your Son Jesus who forgave His persecutors. Today, as I turn away from anger, I will claim the peace that You intend for my life, and I will praise You for Your blessings. Amen

LAUGH!

A cheerful disposition is good for your health;
gloom and doom leave you bone-tired.
Proverbs 17:22 MSG

Laughter is medicine for the soul, but sometimes, amid the stresses of the day, we forget to take our medicine. Instead of viewing our world with a mixture of optimism and humor, we allow worries and distractions to rob us of the joy that God intends for our lives.

So the next time you find yourself dwelling upon the negatives of life, refocus your attention to things positive. And, if you see your glass as "half empty," rest assured that your spiritual vision is impaired. With God, your glass is never half empty. With God as your protector and Christ as your Savior, your glass is filled to the brim and overflowing . . . forever.

Today, as you go about your daily activities, approach life with a smile on your lips and hope in your heart. And laugh every chance you get.

Laughter is like internal jogging—in many ways as good as physical exercise.

Joyce Meyer

We may run, walk, stumble, drive, or fly, but let us never lose sight of the reason for the journey, or miss a chance to see a rainbow on the way.

Gloria Gaither

God is good, and heaven is forever. And if those two facts don't cheer you up, nothing will.

Marie T. Freeman

Laughter dulls the sharpest pain and flattens out the greatest stress. To share it is to give a gift of health.

Barbara Johnson

Wholehearted, ready laughter heals, encourages, relaxes anyone within hearing distance. The laughter that springs from love makes wide the space around it—gives room for the loved one to enter in. Real laughter welcomes, and never shuts out.

Eugenia Price

If you could choose one characteristic that would get you through life, choose a sense of humor.

Jennifer Jones

There is a time for everything, and a season for every activity under heaven . . . a time to weep and a time to laugh, a time to mourn and a time to dance . . . .

Ecclesiastes 3:1,4 NIV

Shout for joy to the LORD, all the earth, burst into jubilant song with music; make music to the LORD with the harp, with the harp and the sound of singing, with trumpets and the blast of the ram's horn—shout for joy before the LORD, the King.

Psalm 98:4-6 NIV

Nehemiah said, "Go and enjoy choice food and sweet drinks, and send some to those who have nothing prepared. This day is sacred to our Lord. Do not grieve, for the joy of the LORD is your strength."

Nehemiah 8:10 NIV

Clap your hands, all you nations; shout to God with cries of joy.

Psalm 47:1 NIV

TODAY'S PRAYER OF GRACE

Dear Lord, You have given me so many reasons to celebrate life. Today, let me be a joyful Christian—quick to smile and quick to laugh. And, let Your love shine in me and through me, this day and forever. Amen

Day 44

Praising God for His Gifts

The Lord reigns; Let the earth rejoice.
Psalm 97:1 NKJV

The Lord intends that believers should share His love with His joy in their hearts. Yet sometimes, amid the inevitable hustle and bustle of life-here-on-earth, we can forfeit—albeit temporarily—God's joy as we wrestle with the challenges of daily living.

Joni Eareckson Tada spoke for Christian women of every generation when she observed, "I wanted the deepest part of me to vibrate with that ancient yet familiar longing, that desire for something that would fill and overflow my soul."

If, today, your heart is heavy, open the door of your soul to Christ. He will give you peace and joy. And if you already have the joy of Christ in your heart, share it freely, just as Christ freely shared His joy with you.

It is the definition of joy to be able to offer back to God the essence of what he's placed in you, be that creativity or a love of ideas or a compassionate heart or the gift of hospitality.

Paula Rinehart

A joyful heart is the inevitable result of a heart burning with love.

Mother Teresa

If you're a thinking Christian, you will be a joyful Christian.

Marie T. Freeman

Finding joy means first of all finding Jesus.

Jill Briscoe

The Christian lifestyle is not one of legalistic do's and don'ts, but one that is positive, attractive, and joyful.

Vonette Bright

Joy is the heart vibrating in grateful rhythm to the love of Almighty God who actually chooses to make His home within us.

Susan Lenzkes

*Weeping may spend the night,
but there is joy in the morning.*

—

Psalm 30:5 HCSB

I have spoken these things to you so that My joy may be in you and your joy may be complete.

John 15:11 HCSB

Rejoice in the Lord always. I will say it again: Rejoice!

Philippians 4:4 HCSB

Delight yourself also in the Lord, and He shall give you the desires of your heart.

Psalm 37:4 NKJV

Make me hear joy and gladness.

Psalm 51:8 NKJV

Today's Prayer of Grace

Dear Lord, You have given me so many blessings; I will celebrate Your gifts. Make me thankful, loving, responsible, and wise. I praise You, Father, for the gift of Your Son and for the priceless gift of salvation. Make me be a joyful Christian, a worthy example to others, and a dutiful servant to You this day and forever. Amen

KINDNESS NOW

Yes indeed, it is good when you truly obey our Lord's
royal command found in the Scriptures:
"Love your neighbor as yourself."

James 2:8 NLT

In the busyness and confusion of daily life, it is easy to lose focus, and it is easy to become frustrated. We are imperfect human beings struggling to manage our lives as best we can, but we often fall short. When we are distracted or disappointed, we may neglect to share a kind word or a kind deed. This oversight hurts others, but it hurts us most of all.

Kindness is a choice. Sometimes, when we feel happy or prosperous, we find it easy to be kind. Other times, when we are discouraged or tired, we can scarcely summon the energy to utter a single kind word. But, God's commandment is clear: we must observe the Golden Rule "in everything." God intends that we make the conscious choice to treat others with kindness and respect, no matter our circumstances, no matter our emotions. Kindness, therefore, is a choice that we, as Christians must make many times each day.

When we weave the thread of kindness into the very fabric of our lives, we give a priceless gift to others, and we give glory to the One who gave His life for us. As believers, we must do no less.

Kindness in this world will do much to help others, not only to come into the light, but also to grow in grace day by day.

Fanny Crosby

Showing kindness to others is one of the nicest things we can do for ourselves.

Janette Oke

Reach out and care for someone who needs the touch of hospitality. The time you spend caring today will be a love gift that will blossom into the fresh joy of God's Spirit in the future.

Emilie Barnes

As much as God loves to hear our worship and adoration, surely he delights all the more in seeing our gratitude translated into simple kindnesses that keep the chain of praise unbroken, alive in others' hearts.

Evelyn Christenson

Sometimes one little spark
of kindness is all it takes to reignite
the light of hope in a heart
that's blinded by pain.

—

Barbara Johnson

Finally, all of you be of one mind, having compassion for one another; love as brothers, be tenderhearted, be courteous.

1 Peter 3:8 NKJV

Love is patient; love is kind.

1 Corinthians 13:4 HCSB

And may the Lord make you increase and abound in love to one another and to all.

1 Thessalonians 3:12 NKJV

And be kind and compassionate to one another, forgiving one another, just as God also forgave you in Christ.

Ephesians 4:32 HCSB

Today's Prayer of Grace

Help me, Lord, to see the needs of those around me. Today, let me show courtesy to those who cross my path. Today, let me spread kind words in honor of Your Son. Today, let forgiveness rule my heart. And every day, Lord, let my love for Christ be demonstrated through the acts of kindness that I offer to those who need the healing touch of the Master's hand. Amen

FINDING COMFORT

Praise be to the God and Father of our Lord Jesus Christ.
God is the Father who is full of mercy and all comfort.
He comforts us every time we have trouble,
so when others have trouble, we can comfort them
with the same comfort God gives us.

2 Corinthians 1:3-4 NCV

A s Christians, we can be assured of this fact: Whether we find ourselves on the pinnacle of the mountain or in the darkest depths of the valley, God is there.

If you have been touched by the transforming love of Jesus, then you have every reason to live courageously. After all, Christ has already won the ultimate battle—and He won it for you—on the cross at Calvary. Still, even if you are a dedicated Christian, you may find yourself discouraged by the inevitable disappointments and tragedies that occur in the lives of believers and non-believers alike.

The next time you find your courage tested to the limit, lean upon God's promises. Trust His Son. Remember that God is always near and that He is your protector and your deliverer. When you are worried, anxious, or afraid, call upon Him and accept the touch of His comforting hand. Remember that God rules both mountaintops and valleys—with limitless wisdom and love—now and forever.

Put your hand into the hand of God.
He gives the calmness and serenity
of heart and soul.

—

Mrs. Charles E. Cowman

Oh! what a Savior, gracious to all, / Oh! how His blessings round us fall, / Gently to comfort, kindly to cheer, / Sleeping or waking, God is near.

Fanny Crosby

O Lord, thank You that Your side of the embroidery of our life is always perfect. That is such a comfort when our side is sometimes so mixed up.

Corrie ten Boom

What a comfort to know that God is present there in your life, available to meet every situation with you, that you are never left to face any problem alone.

Vonette Bright

We all go through pain and sorrow, but the presence of God, like a warm, comforting blanket, can shield us and protect us, and allow the deep inner joy to surface, even in the most devastating circumstances.

Barbara Johnson

When faced with adversity the Christian woman comforts herself with the knowledge that all of life's events are in the hands of God.

Vonette Bright

Carry each other's burdens, and in this way you will fulfill the law of Christ.

Galatians 6:2 NIV

Finally, all of you be of one mind, having compassion for one another; love as brothers, be tenderhearted, be courteous.

1 Peter 3:8 NKJV

So, as those who have been chosen of God, holy and beloved, put on a heart of compassion, kindness, humility, gentleness and patience.

Colossians 3:12 NASB

But he's already made it plain how to live, what to do, what God is looking for in men and women. It's quite simple: Do what is fair and just to your neighbor, be compassionate and loyal in your love, and don't take yourself too seriously—take God seriously.

Micah 6:8 MSG

Today's Prayer of Grace

Today, Lord, let me count my blessings with thanksgiving in my heart. You have cared for me, Lord, and I will give You the glory and the praise. Let me accept Your blessings and Your gifts, and let me share them with others, just as You first shared them with me. Amen

DAY 47

THE GIFT OF LIFE

Seek the Lord, and ye shall live . . . .
Amos 5:6 KJV

L ife is a glorious gift from God. Treat it that way—and while you're at it, praise the Giver for His gift. This day, like every other, is filled to the brim with opportunities, challenges, and choices. But, no choice that you make is more important than the choice you make concerning God. Today, you will either place Him at the center of your life—or not—and the consequences of that choice have implications that are both temporal and eternal.

Sometimes, without our even realizing it, we gradually drift away from the One we need most. Thankfully, God never drifts away from us. He remains always present, always steadfast, always loving.

As you begin this day, place God and His Son where they belong: in your head, in your prayers, on your lips, and in your heart. And then, with God as your guide and companion, let the journey begin . . .

I've finally realized that if something has no significant value, it doesn't deserve my time. Life is not a dress rehearsal, and I'll never get this day again.

Sheri Rose Shepherd

As I contemplate all the sacrifices required in order to live a life that is totally focused on Jesus Christ and His eternal kingdom, the joy seeps out of my heart onto my face in a smile of deep satisfaction.

Anne Graham Lotz

Your life is not a boring stretch of highway. It's a straight line to heaven. And just look at the fields ripening along the way. Look at the tenacity and endurance. Look at the grains of righteousness. You'll have quite a crop at harvest . . . so don't give up!

Joni Eareckson Tada

You have a glorious future in Christ! Live every moment in His power and love.

Vonette Bright

We are common earthenware jars, filled with the treasure of the riches of God. The jar is not important—the treasure is everything.

Corrie ten Boom

And Jesus said unto them,
I am the bread of life:
he that cometh to me
shall never hunger;
and he that believeth on me
shall never thirst.

—

John 6:35 KJV

Watch your life and doctrine closely. Persevere in them, because if you do, you will save both yourself and your hearers.

1 Timothy 4:16 NIV

His divine power has given us everything we need for life and godliness through our knowledge of him who called us by his own glory and goodness.

2 Peter 1:3 NIV

Make it your ambition to lead a quiet life, to mind your own business and to work with your hands, just as we told you, so that your daily life may win the respect of outsiders and so that you will not be dependent on anybody.

1 Thessalonians 4:11-12 NIV

I urge you to live a life worthy of the calling you have received.

Ephesians 4:1 NIV

Today's Prayer of Grace

Lord, You are the Giver of all life. Let me live a life that pleases You, and let me thank You always for Your blessings. You love me and protect me, Heavenly Father. Let me be grateful, and let me live for You today and throughout eternity. Amen

Day 48

HE IS HERE

I am not alone, because the Father is with Me.
John 16:32 HCSB

Since God is everywhere, we are free to sense His presence whenever we take the time to quiet our souls and turn our prayers to Him. But sometimes, amid the incessant demands of everyday life, we turn our thoughts far from God; when we do, we suffer.

Do you set aside quiet moments each day to offer praise to your Creator? As a woman who has received the gift of God's grace, you most certainly should. Silence is a gift that you give to yourself and to God. During these moments of stillness, you will often sense the infinite love and power of your Creator—and He, in turn, will speak directly to your heart.

The familiar words of Psalm 46:10 remind us to "Be still, and know that I am God." When we do so, we encounter the awesome presence of our loving Heavenly Father, and we are comforted in the knowledge that God is not just near. He is here.

It's a crazy world and life speeds by at a blur, yet God is right in the middle of the craziness. And anywhere, at anytime, we may turn to Him, hear His voice, feel His hand, and catch the fragrance of heaven.

Joni Eareckson Tada

We will not fully realize the cost of sin until we finally sit at His feet and know the inexpressible joy of His presence. How can we know what we have lost until we have regained it?

Beth Moore

Oh! what a Savior, gracious to all, / Oh! how His blessings round us fall, / Gently to comfort, kindly to cheer, / Sleeping or waking, God is near.

Fanny Crosby

What God promises is that He always, always comes. He always shows up. He always saves. He always rescues. His timing is not ours. His methods are usually unconventional. But what we can know, what we can settle in our soul, is that He is faithful to come when we call.

Angela Thomas

He is more within us than we are ourselves.

Elizabeth Ann Seton

God walks with us.
He scoops us up in His arms
or simply sits with us in silent
strength until we cannot avoid
the awesome recognition that yes,
even now, He is here.

—

Gloria Gaither

Draw near to God, and He will draw near to you.

James 4:8 HCSB

You will seek Me and find Me when you search for Me with all your heart.

Jeremiah 29:13 HCSB

The Lord is near all who call out to Him, all who call out to Him with integrity. He fulfills the desires of those who fear Him; He hears their cry for help and saves them.

Psalm 145:18-19 HCSB

Surely goodness and mercy shall follow me all the days of my life: and I will dwell in the house of the Lord for ever.

Psalm 23:6 KJV

TODAY'S PRAYER OF GRACE

Dear Lord, You are with me always, and I praise You for Your love. Help me feel Your presence in every situation and every circumstance. Today, Father, I will acknowledge Your presence, Your love, and Your Son. Amen

Day 49

Acceptance Today

One thing I do, forgetting those things which are behind and reaching forward to those things which are ahead,
I press toward the goal for the prize of the upward call of God in Christ Jesus.

Philippians 3:13-14 NKJV

Manmade plans are fallible; God's plans are not. Yet whenever life takes an unexpected turn, we are tempted to fall into the spiritual traps of worry, self-pity, or bitterness. God intends that we do otherwise.

The old saying is familiar: "Forgive and forget." But when we have been hurt badly, forgiveness is often difficult and forgetting is downright impossible. Since we can't forget yesterday's troubles, we should learn from them. Yesterday has much to teach us about tomorrow. We may learn from the past, but we should never live in the past.

So if you're trying to forget the past, don't waste your time. Instead, try a different approach: learn to accept the past and live in the present. Then, you can focus your thoughts and your energies, not on the struggles of yesterday, but instead on the profound opportunities that God has placed before you today.

Acceptance says: True, this is my situation at the moment. I'll look unblinkingly at the reality of it. But, I'll also open my hands to accept willingly whatever a loving Father sends me.

Catherine Marshall

Surrender to the Lord is not a tremendous sacrifice, not an agonizing performance. It is the most sensible thing you can do.

Corrie ten Boom

He does not need to transplant us into a different field. He transforms the very things that were before our greatest hindrances, into the chief and most blessed means of our growth. No difficulties in your case can baffle Him. Put yourself absolutely into His hands, and let Him have His own way with you.

Elisabeth Elliot

I pray hard, work hard, and leave the rest to God.

Florence Griffith Joyner

A man's heart plans his way, but the Lord determines his steps.

Proverbs 16:9 HCSB

For everything created by God is good, and nothing should be rejected if it is received with thanksgiving.

1 Timothy 4:4 HCSB

Should we accept only good from God and not adversity?

Job 2:10 HCSB

He is the Lord. Let him do what he thinks is best.

1 Samuel 3:18 NCV

TODAY'S PRAYER OF GRACE

Lord, when I am discouraged, give me hope. When I am impatient, give me peace. When I face circumstances that I cannot change, give me a spirit of acceptance. In all things great and small, let me trust in You, Dear Lord, knowing that You are the Giver of life and the Giver of all things good, today and forever. Amen

THE RIGHT PRIORITIES

First pay attention to me, and then relax.
Now you can take it easy—you're in good hands.
Proverbs 1:33 MSG

First things first. These words are easy to speak but hard to put into practice. For busy women living in a demanding world, placing first things first can be difficult indeed. Why? Because so many people are expecting so many things from us!

If you're having trouble prioritizing your day, perhaps you've been trying to organize your life according to your own plans, not God's. A better strategy, of course, is to take your daily obligations and place them in the hands of the One who created you. To do so, you must prioritize your day according to God's commandments, and you must seek His will and His wisdom in all matters. Then, you can face the day with the assurance that the same God who created our universe out of nothingness will help you place first things first in your own life.

Do you feel overwhelmed or confused? Turn the concerns of this day over to God—prayerfully, earnestly, and often. Then listen for His answer . . . and trust the answer He gives.

If choosing to spend time alone with God is a real struggle—a heavy-handed demand that only adds more guilt and stress to your already overblown schedule—it's time to change the way you approach his presence.

Doris Greig

Getting things accomplished isn't nearly as important as taking time for love.

Janette Oke

It's sobering to contemplate how much time, effort, sacrifice, compromise, and attention we give to acquiring and increasing our supply of something that is totally insignificant in eternity.

Anne Graham Lotz

Great relief and satisfaction can come from seeking God's priorities for us in each season, discerning what is "best" in the midst of many noble opportunities, and pouring our most excellent energies into those things.

Beth Moore

And I pray this: that your love will keep on growing in knowledge and every kind of discernment, so that you can determine what really matters and can be pure and blameless in the day of Christ.

Philippians 1:9 HCSB

The thing you should want most is God's kingdom and doing what God wants. Then all these other things you need will be given to you.

Matthew 6:33 NCV

He said to them all, "If anyone desires to come after Me, let him deny himself, and take up his cross daily, and follow Me. For whoever desires to save his life will lose it, but whoever loses his life for My sake will save it."

Luke 9:23-24 NKJV

Let us fix our eyes on Jesus, the author and perfecter of our faith, who for the joy set before him endured the cross, scorning its shame, and sat down at the right hand of the throne of God.

Hebrews 12:2 NIV

Today's Prayer of Grace

Dear Lord, let Your priorities be my priorities. Let Your will be my will. Let Your Word be my guide, and let me grow in faith and in wisdom this day and every day. Amen

On Being a Happy Christian

Happy are those who fear the Lord.
Yes, happy are those who delight in doing
what he commands.

Psalm 112:1 NLT

Do you seek happiness, abundance, and contentment? If so, here are some things you should do: Love God and His Son; depend upon God for strength; try, to the best of your abilities, to follow God's will; and strive to obey His Holy Word. When you do these things, you'll discover that happiness goes hand-in-hand with righteousness. The happiest people are not those who rebel against God; the happiest people are those who love God and obey His commandments.

What does life have in store for you? A world full of possibilities (of course it's up to you to seize them) and God's promise of abundance (of course it's up to you to accept it). So, as you embark upon the next phase of your journey, remember to celebrate the life that God has given you. Your Creator has blessed you beyond measure. Honor Him with your prayers, your words, your deeds, and your joy.

When we bring sunshine into the lives of others, we're warmed by it ourselves. When we spill a little happiness, it splashes on us.

Barbara Johnson

When we do what is right, we have contentment, peace, and happiness.

Beverly LaHaye

Christ is the secret, the source, the substance, the center, and the circumference of all true and lasting gladness.

Mrs. Charles E. Cowman

Those who have had to wait and work for happiness seem to enjoy it more, because they never take it for granted.

Barbara Johnson

Those who are God's without reserve are, in every sense, content.

Hannah Whitall Smith

How happy are those whose way is blameless, who live according to the law of the Lord! Happy are those who keep His decrees and seek Him with all their heart.

Psalm 119:1-2 HCSB

If they serve Him obediently, they will end their days in prosperity and their years in happiness.

Job 36:11 HCSB

The one who understands a matter finds success, and the one who trusts in the Lord will be happy.

Proverbs 16:20 HCSB

Happy are the people whose strength is in You, whose hearts are set on pilgrimage.

Psalm 84:5 HCSB

TODAY'S PRAYER OF GRACE

Dear Lord, You are my strength and my joy. I will rejoice in the day that You have made, and I will give thanks for the countless blessings that You have given me. Let me be a joyful Christian, Father, as I share the Good News of Your Son, and let me praise You for all the marvelous things You have done. Amen

Praising God for Heaven

Let not your heart be troubled: ye believe in God,
believe also in me. In my Father's house are many mansions:
if it were not so, I would have told you. I go to prepare a place
for you. And if I go and prepare a place for you,
I will come again, and receive you unto myself;
that where I am, there ye may be also.

John 14:1-3 KJV

Sometimes life's inevitable troubles and heartbreaks are easier to tolerate when we remind ourselves that heaven is our true home. An old hymn contains the words, "This world is not my home; I'm just passing through." Thank goodness!

For believers, death is not an ending; it is a beginning. For believers, the grave is not a final resting-place; it is a place of transition. Death can never claim those who have accepted Christ as their personal Savior. Christ has promised that He has gone to prepare a glorious home in heaven—a timeless, blessed gift to His children—and Jesus always keeps His promises.

If you've committed your life to Christ, your time here on earth is merely a preparation for a far different life to come: your eternal life with Jesus and a host of fellow believers.

So, while this world can be a place of temporary hardship and temporary suffering, you can be comforted in the knowledge that God offers you a permanent home that is free from all suffering and pain. Please take God at His word. When you do, you can withstand any problem, knowing that your troubles are temporary, but that heaven is not.

The end will be glorious beyond
our wildest dreams—for those
who put their trust in Him.

—

Elisabeth Elliot

What joy that the Bible tells us the great comfort that the best is yet to be. Our outlook goes beyond this world.

Corrie ten Boom

Do you know that if at birth I had been able to make one petition, it would have been that I should be born blind? Because, when I get to heaven, the first face that shall ever gladden my sight will be that of my Savior!

Fanny Crosby

One of these days, our Father will scoop us up in His strong arms and we will hear Him say those sweet and comforting words, "Come on, child. We're going home."

Gloria Gaither

The home you've always wanted, the home you continue to long for with all your heart, is the home God is preparing for you!

Anne Graham Lotz

Lord, I thank you for the promise of heaven and the unexpected moments when you touch my heartstrings with that longing for my eternal home.

Joni Eareckson Tada

He also raised us up with Him and seated us with Him in the heavens, in Christ Jesus, so that in the coming ages He might display the immeasurable riches of His grace in His kindness to us in Christ Jesus.

Ephesians 2:6-7 HCSB

Be glad and rejoice, because your reward is great in heaven.

Matthew 5:12 HCSB

Our citizenship is in heaven, from which we also eagerly wait for a Savior, the Lord Jesus Christ.

Philippians 3:20 HCSB

Thy kingdom is an everlasting kingdom, and thy dominion endureth throughout all generations.

Psalm 145:13 KJV

TODAY'S PRAYER OF GRACE

Dear Lord, I praise You for the gift of eternal life that is mine through Your Son Jesus. I will keep the promise of heaven in my heart today and every day. Amen

LISTENING TO GOD

The one who is from God listens to God's words.
This is why you don't listen,
because you are not from God.

John 8:47 HCSB

Sometimes, God displays His wishes in ways that are undeniable. But on other occasions, the hand of God is much more subtle than that. Sometimes, God speaks to us in quiet tones, and when He does, we are well advised to listen . . . carefully.

Do you take time each day for an extended period of silence? And during those precious moments, do you sincerely open your heart to your Creator? If so, you are wise and you are blessed.

The world can be a noisy place, a place filled to the brim with distractions, interruptions, and frustrations. And if you're not careful, the struggles and stresses of everyday living can rob you of the peace that should rightfully be yours because of your personal relationship with Christ. So take time each day to quietly commune with your Savior. When you do, you will most certainly encounter the subtle hand of God, and if you are wise, you will let His hand lead you along the path that He has chosen.

We need to stop focusing on our lacks and stop giving out excuses and start looking at and listening to Jesus.

Anne Graham Lotz

The amazing thing is that God follows us into the blackened ruins of our failed dreams, our misbegotten mirages, into the house of cards that has collapsed on us in some way and he speaks, not with the chastisement we feel we deserve, but of all things, with tenderness.

Paula Rinehart

We need to stop focusing on our lacks and stop giving out excuses and start looking at and listening to Jesus.

Anne Graham Lotz

I have acted like I'm all alone, but the truth is that I never will be. When my prayers are weak, God is listening. When my words are wrote, God is listening. When my heart is dry, amazingly God is still listening.

Angela Thomas

When I am constantly running
there is no time for being.
When there is no time for being
there is no time for listening.

—

Madeleine L'Engle

Listen in silence before me . . . .

Isaiah 41:1 NLT

God has no use for the prayers of the people who won't listen to him.

Proverbs 28:9 MSG

Trust God from the bottom of your heart; don't try to figure out everything on your own. Listen for God's voice in everything you do, everywhere you go; he's the one who will keep you on track.

Proverbs 3:5-6 MSG

You must follow the Lord your God and fear Him. You must keep His commands and listen to His voice; you must worship Him and remain faithful to Him.

Deuteronomy 13:4 HCSB

TODAY'S PRAYER OF GRACE

Dear Lord, I have so much to learn and You have so much to teach me. Give me the wisdom to be still and the discernment to hear Your voice, today and every day. Amen

DAY 54

HE GIVES US HOPE

Without wavering, let us hold tightly to the hope we say we have, for God can be trusted to keep his promise.

Hebrews 10:23 NLT

Despite God's promises, despite Christ's love, and despite our countless blessings, we frail human beings can still lose hope from time to time. When we do, we need the encouragement of Christian friends, the life-changing power of prayer, and the healing truth of God's Holy Word.

If you find yourself falling into the spiritual traps of worry and discouragement, seek the healing touch of Jesus and the encouraging words of fellow Christians. And remember the words of our Savior: "These things I have spoken unto you, that in me ye might have peace. In the world ye shall have tribulation: but be of good cheer; I have overcome the world" (John 16:33 KJV). This world can be a place of trials and tribulations, but as believers, we are secure. God has promised us peace, joy, and eternal life. And, of course, God keeps His promises today, tomorrow, and forever.

No other religion, no other philosophy promises new bodies, hearts, and minds. Only in the Gospel of Christ do hurting people find such incredible hope.

Joni Eareckson Tada

In those desperate times when we feel like we don't have an ounce of strength, He will gently pick up our heads so that our eyes can behold something—something that will keep His hope alive in us.

Kathy Troccoli

The choice for me is to either look at all things I have lost or the things I have. To live in fear or to live in hope.... Hope comes from knowing I have a sovereign, loving God who is in every event in my life.

Lisa Beamer(Her husband Todd was killed on flight 93, 9-11-01)

Love is the seed of all hope. It is the enticement to trust, to risk, to try, and to go on.

Gloria Gaither

I discovered that sorrow was not to be feared but rather endured with hope and expectancy that God would use it to visit and bless my life.

Jill Briscoe

For I know the thoughts that I think toward you, says the Lord, thoughts of peace and not of evil, to give you a future and a hope. Then you will call upon Me and go and pray to Me, and I will listen to you.

Jeremiah 29:11-12 NKJV

Hope deferred makes the heart sick.

Proverbs 13:12 NKJV

Sustain me as You promised, and I will live; do not let me be ashamed of my hope.

Psalm 119:116 HCSB

Be of good courage, and He shall strengthen your heart, all you who hope in the Lord.

Psalm 31:24 NKJV

Today's Prayer of Grace

Dear Lord, make me a woman of hope. If I become discouraged, let me turn to You. If I grow weary, let me seek strength in You. When I face disappointments, let me seek Your will and trust Your Word. In every aspect of my life, I will trust You, Father, so that my heart will be filled with faith, hope, and praise, this day and forever. Amen

MAKING PEACE WITH THE PAST

I do not consider myself yet to have taken hold of it.
But one thing I do: Forgetting what is behind and straining
toward what is ahead, I press on toward the goal
to win the prize for which God has called me
heavenward in Christ Jesus.

Philippians 3:13-14 NIV

The American theologian Reinhold Niebuhr composed a profoundly simple verse that came to be known as the Serenity Prayer: "God, grant me the serenity to accept the things I cannot change, the courage to change the things I can, and the wisdom to know the difference." Niebuhr's words are far easier to recite than they are to live by. Why? Because most of us want life to unfold in accordance with our own wishes and timetables. But sometimes God has other plans.

One of the things that fits nicely into the category of "things we cannot change" is the past. Yet even though we know that the past is unchangeable, many of us continue to invest energy worrying about the unfairness of yesterday (when we should, instead, be focusing on the opportunities of today and the promises of tomorrow). Author Hannah Whitall Smith observed, "How changed our lives would be if we could only fly through the days on wings of surrender and trust!" These words remind us that even when we cannot understand the past, we must trust God and accept His will.

So, if you've endured a difficult past, accept it and learn from it, but don't spend too much time here in the precious present fretting over memories of the unchangeable past. Instead, trust God's plan and look to the future. After all, the future is where everything that's going to happen to you from this moment on is going to take place.

We need to be at peace with our past, content with our present, and sure about our future, knowing they are all in God's hands.

Joyce Meyer

Our yesterdays teach us how to savor our todays and tomorrows.

Patsy Clairmont

If you are God's child, you are no longer bound to your past or to what you were. You are a brand new creature in Christ Jesus.

Kay Arthur

Shake the dust from your past, and move forward in His promises.

Kay Arthur

No matter what, don't ever let yesterday use up too much of today.

Barbara Johnson

We can't just put our pasts behind us. We've got to put our pasts in front of God.

Beth Moore

Do not remember the past events, pay no attention to things of old. Look, I am about to do something new; even now it is coming. Do you not see it? Indeed, I will make a way in the wilderness, rivers in the desert.

Isaiah 43:18-19 HCSB

Your old life is dead. Your new life, which is your real life—even though invisible to spectators—is with Christ in God. He is your life.

Colossians 3:3 MSG

Create in me a pure heart, O God, and renew a steadfast spirit within me.

Psalm 51:10 NIV

And He who sits on the throne said, "Behold, I am making all things new."

Revelation 21:5 NASB

TODAY'S PRAYER OF GRACE

Heavenly Father, free me from anger, resentment, and envy. When I am bitter, I cannot feel the peace that You intend for my life. Keep me mindful that forgiveness is Your commandment, and help me accept the past, treasure the present, and trust the future . . . to You. Amen

HE IS YOUR ROCK

The Lord is my rock and my fortress and my deliverer;
the God of my strength, in whom I will trust.

2 Samuel 22:2-3 NKJV

God has promised to protect us, and He intends to keep His promise. In a world filled with dangers and temptations, God is the ultimate armor. In a world filled with misleading messages, God's Word is the ultimate truth. In a world filled with more frustrations than we can count, God's Son offers the ultimate peace.

As a busy woman, you know from firsthand experience that life is not always easy. But as a recipient of God's grace, you also know that you are protected by a loving Heavenly Father.

In times of trouble, God will comfort you; in times of sorrow, He will dry your tears. When you are troubled, weak, or sorrowful, God is neither distant nor disinterested. To the contrary, God is always present and always vitally engaged in the events of your life. Reach out to Him, and build your future on the rock that cannot be shaken. He can provide everything you really need.

God provides the ingredients for our daily bread but expects us to do the baking. With our own hands!

Barbara Johnson

He goes before us, follows behind us, and hems us safe inside the realm of His protection.

Beth Moore

We can take great comfort that God never sleeps—so we can.

Dianna Booher

God will never let you sink under your circumstances. He always provide a safety net and His love always encircles.

Barbara Johnson

When you live a surrendered life, God is willing and able to provide for your every need.

Corrie ten Boom

Our God is the sovereign Creator of the universe! He loves us as His own children and has provided every good thing we have; He is worthy of our praise every moment.

Shirley Dobson

I know whom I have believed and am persuaded that He is able to guard what has been entrusted to me until that day.

2 Timothy 1:12 HCSB

For the LORD your God has arrived to live among you. He is a mighty Savior. He will rejoice over you with great gladness. With his love, he will calm all your fears. He will exult over you by singing a happy song.

Zephaniah 3:17 HCSB

God—His way is perfect; the word of the Lord is pure. He is a shield to all who take refuge in Him.

Psalm 18:30 HCSB

The Lord is my rock, my fortress, and my deliverer.

Psalm 18:2 HCSB

TODAY'S PRAYER OF GRACE

Lord, You are my Shepherd. You care for me; You comfort me; You watch over me; and You have saved me. I will praise You, Father, for Your glorious works, for Your protection, for Your love, and for Your Son. Amen

Today's Theme: Path

WALKING ON HIS PATH

*Then He said to them all, "If anyone desires to come
after Me, let him deny himself, and take up his cross daily,
and follow Me. For whoever desires to save his life will lose it,
but whoever loses his life for My sake will save it."*

Luke 9:23-24 NKJV

When Jesus addressed His disciples, He warned that each one must, "take up his cross and follow me." The disciples must have known exactly what the Master meant. In Jesus' day, prisoners were forced to carry their own crosses to the location where they would be put to death. Thus, Christ's message was clear: in order to follow Him, Christ's disciples must deny themselves and, instead, trust Him completely. Nothing has changed since then.

If we are to be dutiful disciples of the One from Galilee, we must trust Him and we must follow Him. Jesus never comes "next." He is always first. He shows us the path of life.

Do you seek to be a worthy disciple of Jesus? Then pick up His cross today and follow in His footsteps. When you do, you can walk with confidence: He will never lead you astray.

We are all on our way somewhere.
We'll get there
if we just keep going.

—

Barbara Johnson

We cannot always understand the ways of Almighty God—the crosses which he sends us, the sacrifices which he demands of us. But, if we accept with faith and resignation his holy will—with no looking back to what might have been—we are at peace.

Rose Fitzgerald Kennedy

The Christian faith is meant to be lived moment by moment. It isn't some broad, general outline—it's a long walk with a real Person. Details count: passing thoughts, small sacrifices, a few encouraging words, little acts of kindness, brief victories over nagging sins.

Joni Eareckson Tada

The cross that Jesus commands you and me to carry is the cross of submissive obedience to the will of God, even when His will includes suffering and hardship and things we don't want to do.

Anne Graham Lotz

Choose Jesus Christ! Deny yourself, take up the Cross, and follow Him—for the world must be shown. The world must see, in us, a discernible, visible, startling difference.

Elisabeth Elliot

But whoever keeps His word, truly in him the love of God is perfected. This is how we know we are in Him: the one who says he remains in Him should walk just as He walked.

1 John 2:5-6 HCSB

However, I did give them this command: Obey Me, and then I will be your God, and you will be My people. You must walk in every way I command you so that it may go well with you.

Jeremiah 7:23 HCSB

Keep your eyes focused on what is right, and look straight ahead to what is good. Be careful what you do, and always do what is right. Don't turn off the road of goodness; keep away from evil paths.

Proverbs 4:25-27 NCV

Today's Prayer of Grace

Lord, sometimes life is difficult. But even when I can't see any hope for the future, You are always with me. And, I can live courageously because I know that You are leading me to a place where I can accomplish Your kingdom's work . . . and where You lead, I will follow. Amen

BEYOND PESSIMISM

*Why are you cast down, O my soul? And why are you
disquieted within me? Hope in God; for I shall yet praise
Him, the help of my countenance and my God.*

Psalm 42:11 NKJV

Pessimism and Christianity don't mix. Why? Because
Christians have every reason to be optimistic about
life here on earth and life eternal.

Sometimes, despite our trust in God, we may fall into
the spiritual traps of worry, frustration, anxiety, or sheer
exhaustion, and our hearts become heavy. What's needed
is plenty of rest, a large dose of perspective, and God's
healing touch, but not necessarily in that order.

Today, make this promise to yourself and keep it:
vow to be a hope-filled Christian. Think optimistically
about your life, your profession, and your future. Trust
your hopes, not your fears. Take time to celebrate God's
glorious creation. And then, when you've filled your heart
with hope and gladness, share your optimism with others.
They'll be better for it, and so will you. But not necessarily
in that order.

Worry is the darkroom in which negatives are developed.

Anonymous

God's Word never said we were not to grieve our losses. It says we are not to grieve as those who have no hope (1 Thessalonians 4:13). Big Difference.

Beth Moore

Never yield to gloomy anticipation. Place your hope and confidence in God. He has no record of failure.

Mrs. Charles E. Cowman

When we look at the individual parts of our lives, some things appear unfair and unpleasant. When we take them out of the context of the big picture, we easily drift into the attitude that we deserve better, and the tumble down into the pit of pride begins.

Susan Hunt

A pessimist is someone who believes that when her cup runneth over she'll need a mop.

Barbara Johnson

We never get anywhere—nor do our conditions and circumstances change—when we look at the dark side of life.

Mrs. Charles E. Cowman

We also have joy with our troubles, because we know that these troubles produce patience. And patience produces character, and character produces hope.

Romans 5:3-4 NCV

Think of yourselves the way Christ Jesus thought of himself. He had equal status with God but didn't think so much of himself that he had to cling to the advantages of that status no matter what. Not at all. When the time came, he set aside the privileges of deity and took on the status of a slave, became human! Having become human, he stayed human. It was an incredibly humbling process. He didn't claim special privileges. Instead he lived a selfless, obedient life and then died a selfless, obedient death, and the worst kind of death at that: a crucifixion.

Philippians 2:5-8 MSG

Today's Prayer of Grace

Dear Heavenly Father, on those days when I am troubled, You comfort me if I turn my thoughts and prayers to You. When I am afraid, You protect me. When I am discouraged, You lift me up. You are my unending source of strength, Lord. In every circumstance, let me trust Your plan and Your will for my life. Amen

THE POWER OF PATIENCE

*The Lord is wonderfully good to those who wait for him
and seek him. So it is good to wait quietly
for salvation from the Lord.*

Lamentations 3:25-26 NLT

A re you a woman in a hurry? If so, you may be in for a few disappointments. Why? Because life has a way of unfolding according to its own timetable, not yours. That's why life requires patience . . . and lots of it!

Most of us are impatient for God to grant us the desires of our heart. Usually, we know what we want, and we know precisely when we want it: right now, if not sooner. But God may have other plans. And when God's plans differ from our own, we must trust in His infinite wisdom and in His infinite love.

Lamentations 3:25 reminds us that, "The Lord is wonderfully good to those who wait for him and seek him" (NIV). But, for most of us, waiting quietly is difficult because we're in such a hurry for things to happen!

The next time you find your patience tested to the limit, slow down, take a deep breath, and relax. Sometimes life can't be hurried—and during those times, patience is indeed a priceless virtue.

How do you wait upon the Lord? First you must learn to sit at His feet and take time to listen to His words.

Kay Arthur

We must learn to wait. There is grace supplied to the one who waits.

Mrs. Charles E. Cowman

Let me encourage you to continue to wait with faith. God may not perform a miracle, but He is trustworthy to touch you and make you whole where there used to be a hole.

Lisa Whelchel

Waiting is the hardest kind of work, but God knows best, and we may joyfully leave all in His hands.

Lottie Moon

Wisdom always waits for the right time to act, while emotion always pushes for action right now.

Joyce Meyer

Rejoice in hope; be patient in affliction; be persistent in prayer.

Romans 12:12 HCSB

Love is patient; love is kind.

1 Corinthians 13:4 HCSB

A patient spirit is better than a proud spirit.

Ecclesiastes 7:8 HCSB

Therefore the Lord is waiting to show you mercy, and is rising up to show you compassion, for the Lord is a just God. Happy are all who wait patiently for Him.

Isaiah 30:18 HCSB

Today's Prayer of Grace

Lord, give me patience. When I am hurried, give me peace. When I am frustrated, give me perspective. When I am angry, let me turn my heart to You. Today, let me become a more patient woman, Dear Lord, as I trust in You and in Your master plan for my life. Amen

PRAISING GOD FOR HIS PERFECT TIMING

Therefore humble yourselves under the mighty hand of God,
that He may exalt you in due time.
1 Peter 5:6 NKJV

If you sincerely seek to be a woman of faith, then you must learn to trust God's timing. You will be sorely tempted, however, to do otherwise. Because you are a fallible human being, you are impatient for things to happen. But, God knows better.

God has created a world that unfolds according to His own timetable, not ours . . . thank goodness! We mortals might make a terrible mess of things. God does not.

God's plan does not always happen in the way that we would like or at the time of our own choosing. Our task—as believing Christians who trust in a benevolent, all-knowing Father—is to wait patiently for God to reveal Himself. And reveal Himself He will. Always. But until God's perfect plan is made known, we must walk in faith and never lose hope. And we must continue to trust Him. Always.

God manages perfectly, day and night, year in and year out, the movements of the stars, the wheeling of the planets, the staggering coordination of events that goes on at the molecular level in order to hold things together. There is no doubt that He can manage the timing of my days and weeks.

Elisabeth Elliot

When we read of the great Biblical leaders, we see that it was not uncommon for God to ask them to wait, not just a day or two, but for years, until God was ready for them to act.

Gloria Gaither

We must leave it to God to answer our prayers in His own wisest way. Sometimes, we are so impatient and think that God does not answer. God always answers! He never fails! Be still. Abide in Him.

Mrs. Charles E. Cowman

What God promises is that He always, always comes. He always shows up. He always saves. He always rescues. His timing is not ours. His methods are usually unconventional. But what we can know, what we can settle in our soul, is that He is faithful to come when we call.

Angela Thomas

Waiting on God brings us
to the journey's end quicker
than our feet.

—

Mrs. Charles E. Cowman

He said to them, "It is not for you to know times or periods that the Father has set by His own authority."

Acts 1:7 HCSB

To everything there is a season, a time for every purpose under heaven.

Ecclesiastes 3:1 NKJV

Therefore the Lord is waiting to show you mercy, and is rising up to show you compassion, for the Lord is a just God. Happy are all who wait patiently for Him.

Isaiah 30:18 HCSB

I waited patiently for the LORD; and He inclined to me, and heard my cry.

Psalm 40:1 NKJV

TODAY'S PRAYER OF GRACE

Dear Lord, Your wisdom is infinite, and the timing of Your heavenly plan is perfect. You have a plan for my life that is grander than I can imagine. When I am impatient, remind me that You are never early or late. You are always on time, Father, so let me trust in You. Amen

DAY 61

TRUSTING GOD'S WILL

Teach me to do Your will, for You are my God;
Your Spirit is good. Lead me in the land of uprightness.
Psalm 143:10 NKJV

The Book of Judges tells the story of Deborah, the fearless woman who helped lead the army of Israel to victory over the Canaanites. Deborah was a judge and a prophetess, a woman called by God to lead her people. And when she answered God's call, she was rewarded with one of the great victories of Old Testament times.

Like Deborah, all of us are called to serve our Creator. And, like Deborah, we may sometimes find ourselves facing trials that can bring trembling to the very depths of our souls. As believers, we must seek God's will and follow it. When we do, we are reward with victories, some great and some small. When we entrust our lives to Him completely and without reservation, He gives us the strength to meet any challenge, the courage to face any trial, and the wisdom to live in His righteousness and in His peace.

The only safe place is in the center of God's will. It is not only the safest place. It is also the most rewarding and the most satisfying place to be.

Gigi Graham Tchividjian

Obedience is a foundational stepping stone on the path of God's Will.

Elizabeth George

I believe that in every time and place it is within our power to acquiesce in the will of God—and what peace it brings to do so!

Elisabeth Elliot

The center of power is not to be found in summit meetings or in peace conferences. It is not in Peking or Washington or the United Nations, but rather where a child of God prays in the power of the Spirit for God's will to be done in her life, in her home, and in the world around her.

Ruth Bell Graham

In the Garden of Gethsemane, Jesus went through agony of soul in His efforts to resist the temptation to do what He felt like doing rather than what He knew was God's will for Him.

Joyce Meyer

The will of God
is the most delicious and
delightful thing in the universe.

—

Hannah Whitall Smith

He is the Lord. He will do what He thinks is good.

1 Samuel 3:18 HCSB

Teach me your ways, O LORD, that I may live according to your truth! Grant me purity of heart, that I may honor you.

Psalm 86:11 NLT

Commit your activities to the Lord and your plans will be achieved.

Proverbs 16:3 HCSB

And this world is fading away, along with everything it craves. But if you do the will of God, you will live forever.

1 John 2:17 NLT

TODAY'S PRAYER OF GRACE

Lord, let Your will be my will. When I am confused, give me maturity and wisdom. When I am worried, give me courage and strength. Let me be Your faithful servant, Father, always seeking Your guidance and Your will for my life. Amen

THE VALUE OF WORK

Therefore by their fruits you will know them.
Matthew 7:20 NKJV

God's Word teaches us the value of hard work. In his second letter to the Thessalonians, Paul warns, " …if any would not work, neither should he eat" (3:10 KJV). And the Book of Proverbs proclaims, "One who is slack in his work is brother to one who destroys" (18:9 NIV). In short, God has created a world in which diligence is rewarded but sloth is not. So, whatever it is that you choose to do, do it with commitment, excitement, and vigor.

Hard work is not simply a proven way to get ahead, it's also part of God's plan for you. God did not create you for a life of mediocrity; He created you for far greater things. Reaching for greater things usually requires work and lots of it, which is perfectly fine with God. After all, He knows that you're up to the task, and He has big plans for you if you possess a loving heart and willing hands.

In the very place where God has put us, whatever its limitations, whatever kind of work it may be, we may indeed serve the Lord Christ.

Elisabeth Elliot

If you honor God with your work, He will honor you because of your work.

Marie T. Freeman

God provides the ingredients for our daily bread but expects us to do the baking. With our own hands!

Barbara Johnson

Ordinary work, which is what most of us do most of the time, is ordained by God every bit as much as is the extraordinary.

Elisabeth Elliot

You can't climb the ladder of life with your hands in your pockets.

Barbara Johnson

Great relief and satisfaction can come from seeking God's priorities for us in each season, discerning what is "best" in the midst of many noble opportunities, and pouring our most excellent energies into those things.

Beth Moore

Even Jesus, clear as he was about his calling, had to get his instructions one day at a time. One time he was told to wait, another time to go.

—

Laurie Beth Jones

In fact, when we were with you, this is what we commanded you: "If anyone isn't willing to work, he should not eat."

2 Thessalonians 3:10 HCSB

Be strong and courageous, and do the work.

1 Chronicles 28:20 HCSB

Now the one who plants and the one who waters are equal, and each will receive his own reward according to his own labor.

1 Corinthians 3:8 HCSB

For we are God's co-workers. You are God's field, God's building.

1 Corinthians 3:9 HCSB

Today's Prayer of Grace

Heavenly Father, I seek to be Your faithful servant. When I am tired, give me strength. When I become frustrated, give me patience. When I lose sight of Your purpose for my life, give me a passion for my daily responsibilities, and when I have completed my work, let all the honor and glory be Yours. Amen

Today's Theme: God's Sufficiency

HIS GRACE IS SUFFICIENT

My grace is sufficient for you,
for My strength is made perfect in weakness.
2 Corinthians 12:9 NKJV

O f this you can be sure: the loving heart of God is sufficient to meet your needs. Whatever dangers you may face, whatever heartbreaks you must endure, God is with you, and He stands ready to comfort you and to heal you.

The Psalmist writes, "Weeping may endure for a night, but joy comes in the morning" (Psalm 30:5 NKJV). But when we are suffering, the morning may seem very far away. It is not. God promises that He is "near to those who have a broken heart" (Psalm 34:18 NKJV). In times of intense sadness, we must turn to Him, and we must encourage our friends and family members to do likewise.

If you are experiencing the intense pain of a recent loss, or if you are still mourning a loss from long ago, perhaps you are now ready to begin the next stage of your journey with God. If so, be mindful of this fact: the loving heart of God is sufficient to meet any challenge, including yours. Trust the sufficient heart of God.

God is always sufficient
in perfect proportion to our need.

—

Beth Moore

God's saints in all ages have realized that God was enough for them. God is enough for time; God is enough for eternity. God is enough!

Hannah Whitall Smith

I grew up learning to be self-reliant, but now, to grow up in Christ, I must unlearn self-reliance and learn self-distrust in light of his all-sufficiency.

Mary Morrison Suggs

Snuggle in God's arms. When you are hurting, when you feel lonely or left out, let Him cradle you, comfort you, reassure you of His all-sufficient power and love.

Kay Arthur

Like Paul, we may bear thorns so that we can discover God's perfect sufficiency.

Beth Moore

The last and greatest lesson that the soul has to learn is the fact that God, and God alone, is enough for all its needs. This is the lesson that all His dealings with us are meant to teach; and this is the crowning discovery of our whole Christian life. God is enough!

Hannah Whitall Smith

When God wanted to guarantee his promises, he gave his word, a rock-solid guarantee. God can't break his word. And because his word cannot change, the promise is likewise unchangeable. It's an unbreakable spiritual lifeline, reaching past all appearances right to the very presence of God.

Hebrews 6:17-19 MSG

And God is able to make all grace abound to you, so that always having all sufficiency in everything, you may have an abundance for every good deed;

2 Corinthians 9:8 NASB

For His divine power has given us everything required for life and godliness, through the knowledge of Him who called us by His own glory and goodness.

2 Peter 1:3 HCSB

TODAY'S PRAYER OF GRACE

Dear Lord, You are sufficient for my needs, and I praise You. I will turn to You when I am fearful or worried. You are my loving Heavenly Father, sufficient in all things and I will always trust You. Amen

DAY 64

BEYOND WORRY

Worry is a heavy load . . . .
Proverbs 12:25 NCV

"Worry does not empty tomorrow of its sorrow; it empties today of its strength." So writes Corrie ten Boom, a woman who survived a Nazi concentration camp during World War II. And while our own situations cannot be compared to Corrie's, we still worry about countless matters both great and small. Even though we are Christians who have been given the assurance of salvation—even though we are Christians who have received the promise of God's love and protection—we find ourselves fretting over the countless details of everyday life. Jesus understood our concerns when He spoke the reassuring words found in Matthew 6: "Therefore I tell you, do not worry about your life . . ."

As you consider the promises of Jesus, remember that God still sits in His heaven and you are His beloved child. Then, perhaps, you will worry a little less and trust God a little more, and that's as it should be because God is trustworthy . . . and you are protected.

Never yield to gloomy anticipation. Place your hope and confidence in God. He has no record of failure.

Mrs. Charles E. Cowman

Worries carry responsibilities that belong to God, not to you. Worry does not enable us to escape evil; it makes us unfit to cope with it when it comes.

Corrie ten Boom

Worry is the senseless process of cluttering up tomorrow's opportunities with leftover problems from today.

Barbara Johnson

We are meddling with God's business when we let all manner of imaginings loose, predicting disaster, contemplating possibilities instead of following, one day at a time, God's plain and simple pathway.

Elisabeth Elliot

Remember always that there are two things which are more utterly incompatible even than oil and water, and these two are trust and worry.

Hannah Whitall Smith

Worship and worry
cannot live in the same heart;
they are mutually exclusive.

—

Ruth Bell Graham

Don't worry about anything, but in everything, through prayer and petition with thanksgiving, let your requests be made known to God.

Philippians 4:6 HCSB

Don't worry about your life, what you will eat or what you will drink; or about your body, what you will wear. Isn't life more than food and the body more than clothing?

Matthew 6:25 HCSB

I will be with you when you pass through the waters . . . when you walk through the fire . . . the flame will not burn you. For I the Lord your God, the Holy One of Israel, and your Savior.

Isaiah 43:2-3 HCSB

TODAY'S PRAYER OF GRACE

Lord, You sent Your Son to live as a man on this earth, and You know what it means to be completely human. You understand my worries and my fears, Lord, and You forgive me when I am weak. When my faith begins to wane, help me, Lord, to trust You more. Then, with Your Holy Word on my lips and with the love of Your Son in my heart, let me live courageously, faithfully, prayerfully, and thankfully today and every day. Amen

Worship Him

For it is written, "You shall worship the Lord your God,
and Him only you shall serve."

Matthew 4:10 NKJV

All of mankind is engaged in the practice of worship. Some choose to worship God and, as a result, reap the joy that He intends for His children. Others distance themselves from God by worshiping such things as earthly possessions or personal gratification . . . and when they do so, they suffer.

Today, as one way of worshipping God, make every aspect of your life a cause for celebration and praise. Praise God for the blessings and opportunities that He has given you, and live according to the beautiful words found in the 5th chapter of 1 Thessalonians: "Rejoice evermore. Pray without ceasing. In every thing give thanks: for this is the will of God in Christ Jesus concerning you" (vv. 16-18 KJV).

God deserves your worship, your prayers, your praise, and your thanks. And you deserve the joy that is yours when you worship Him with your prayers, with your deeds, and with your life.

Worship always empowers the worshiper with a greater revelation of the object of her desire.

Lisa Bevere

It's our privilege to not only raise our hands in worship but also to combine the visible with the invisible in a rising stream of praise and adoration sent directly to our Father.

Shirley Dobson

God has promised to give you all of eternity. The least you can do is give Him one day a week in return.

Marie T. Freeman

God asks that we worship Him with our concentrated minds as well as with our wills and emotions. A divided and scattered mind is not effective.

Catherine Marshall

To worship Him in truth means to worship Him honestly, without hypocrisy, standing open and transparent before Him.

Anne Graham Lotz

Worship is God-centered, aware of one another only in that deep, joyous awareness of being caught up together in God.

Anne Ortlund

*For where two or three
are gathered together in My name,
I am there among them.*

—

Matthew 18:20 HCSB

I rejoiced with those who said to me, "Let us go to the house of the Lord."

Psalm 122:1 HCSB

And every day they devoted themselves to meeting together in the temple complex, and broke bread from house to house. They ate their food with gladness and simplicity of heart, praising God and having favor with all the people. And every day the Lord added those being saved to them.

Acts 2:46-47 HCSB

But an hour is coming, and is now here, when the true worshipers will worship the Father in spirit and truth. Yes, the Father wants such people to worship Him. God is Spirit, and those who worship Him must worship in spirit and truth.

John 4:23-24 HCSB

TODAY'S PRAYER OF GRACE

When I worship You, Lord, You direct my path and You cleanse my heart. Let today and every day be a time of worship and praise. Let me worship You in everything that I think and do. Thank You, Lord, for the priceless gift of Your Son Jesus. Let me be worthy of that gift, and let me give You the praise and the glory forever. Amen

DAY 66

DOING IT NOW, NOT LATER

Are there those among you who are truly wise and understanding? Then they should show it by living right and doing good things with a gentleness that comes from wisdom.

James 3:13 NCV

The old saying is both familiar and true: actions speak louder than words. And as believers, we must beware: our actions should always give credence to the changes that Christ can make in the lives of those who walk with Him.

God calls upon each of us to act in accordance with His will and with respect for His commandments. If we are to be responsible believers, we must realize that it is never enough simply to hear the instructions of God; we must also live by them. And it is never enough to wait idly by while others do God's work here on earth; we, too, must act. Doing God's work is a responsibility that each of us must bear, and when we do, our loving Heavenly Father rewards our efforts with a bountiful harvest.

God has lots of folks who intend to go to work for Him "some day." What He needs is more people who are willing to work for Him this day.

Marie T. Freeman

Every word we speak, every action we take, has an effect on the totality of humanity. No one can escape that privilege—or that responsibility.

Laurie Beth Jones

Slowly I have realized that I do not have to be qualified to do what I am asked to do, that I just have to go ahead and do it, even if I can't do it as well as I think it ought to be done. This is one of the most liberating lessons of my life.

Madeleine L'Engle

A bird does not know it can fly before it uses its wings. We learn God's love in our hearts as soon as we act upon it.

Corrie ten Boom

From the very moment one feels called to act is born the strength to bear whatever horror one will feel or see. In some inexplicable way, terror loses its overwhelming power when it becomes a task that must be faced.

Emmi Bonhoeffer

We spend our lives dreaming of
the future, not realizing that
a little of it slips away every day.

—

Barbara Johnson

For the Kingdom of God is not just fancy talk; it is living by God's power.

1 Corinthians 4:20 NLT

Therefore, get your minds ready for action, being self-disciplined, and set your hope completely on the grace to be brought to you at the revelation of Jesus Christ.

1 Peter 1:13 HCSB

But prove yourselves doers of the word, and not merely hearers.

James 1:22 NASB

The prudent see danger and take refuge, but the simple keep going and suffer from it.

Proverbs 27:12 NIV

TODAY'S PRAYER OF GRACE

Dear Lord, I have heard Your Word, and I have felt Your presence in my heart; let me act accordingly. Let my words and deeds serve as a testimony to the changes You have made in my life. Today, I will praise You, Father, by following in the footsteps of Your Son, and letting others see Him through me. Amen

The Power of Perseverance

If you do nothing in a difficult time, your strength is limited.
Proverbs 24:10 HCSB

In a world filled with roadblocks and stumbling blocks, we need strength, courage, and perseverance. And, as an example of perfect perseverance, we need look no further than our Savior, Jesus Christ.

Jesus finished what He began. Despite the torture He endured, despite the shame of the cross, Jesus was steadfast in His faithfulness to God. We, too, must remain faithful, especially during times of hardship.

Perhaps you are in a hurry for God to reveal His plans for your life. If so, be forewarned: God operates on His own timetable, not yours. Sometimes, God may answer your prayers with silence, and when He does, you must patiently persevere. In times of trouble, you must remain steadfast and trust in the merciful goodness of your Heavenly Father. Whatever your problem, He can handle it. Your job is to keep persevering until He does.

We ought to make some progress, however little, every day, and show some increase of fervor. We ought to act as if we were at war—as, indeed, we are—and never relax until we have won the victory.

St. Teresa of Avila

Are you a Christian? If you are, how can you be hopeless? Are you so depressed by the greatness of your problems that you have given up all hope? Instead of giving up, would you patiently endure? Would you focus on Christ until you are so preoccupied with him alone that you fall prostrate before him?

Anne Graham Lotz

Failure is one of life's most powerful teachers. How we handle our failures determines whether we're going to simply "get by" in life or "press on."

Beth Moore

Your life is not a boring stretch of highway. It's a straight line to heaven. And just look at the fields ripening along the way. Look at the tenacity and endurance. Look at the grains of righteousness. You'll have quite a crop at harvest . . . so don't give up!

Joni Eareckson Tada

We can do anything we want to do
if we stick to it long enough.

—

Helen Keller

I leave you peace; my peace I give you. I do not give it to you as the world does. So don't let your hearts be troubled or afraid.

John 14:27 NCV

If your sinful nature controls your mind, there is death. But if the Holy Spirit controls your mind, there is life and peace.

Romans 8:6 NLT

And the peace of God, which surpasses all understanding, will guard your hearts and minds through Christ Jesus. Finally, brethren, whatever things are true, whatever things are noble, whatever things are just, whatever things are pure, whatever things are lovely, whatever things are of good report, if there is any virtue and if there is anything praiseworthy—meditate on these things.

Philippians 4:7-8 NKJV

Today's Prayer of Grace

Lord, when life is difficult, I am tempted to abandon hope in the future. But You are my God, and I can draw strength from You. Let me trust You, Father, in good times and in bad times. Let me persevere—even if my soul is troubled—and let me follow Your Son, Jesus Christ, this day and forever. Amen

The Cornerstone

The Lord is the strength of my life.

Psalm 27:1 KJV

Have you made God the cornerstone of your life, or is He relegated to a few hours on Sunday morning? Have you genuinely allowed God to reign over every corner of your heart, or have you attempted to place Him in a spiritual compartment? The answer to these questions will determine the direction of your day and your life.

God loves you. In times of trouble, He will comfort you; in times of sorrow, He will dry your tears. When you are weak or sorrowful, God is as near as your next breath. He stands at the door of your heart and waits. Welcome Him in and allow Him to rule. And then, accept the peace, the strength, the protection, and the abundance that only God can give.

You are mighty, Lord, you are mighty. Nothing compares to you in power. No one can equal the strength of your hand.

Mary Morrison Suggs

Measure the size of the obstacles against the size of God.

Beth Moore

So rejoice! You are giving Him what He asks you to give Him—the chance to show you what He can do.

Amy Carmichael

He goes before us, follows behind us, and hems us safe inside the realm of His protection.

Beth Moore

God will never lead you where His strength cannot keep you.

Barbara Johnson

God walks with us. He scoops us up in His arms or simply sits with us in silent strength until we cannot avoid the awesome recognition that yes, even now, He is here.

Gloria Gaither

But the Lord is faithful; he will make you strong and guard you from the evil one.

2 Thessalonians 3:3 NLT

I can do all things through Christ which strengtheneth me.

Philippians 4:13 KJV

You are the God who works wonders; You revealed Your strength among the peoples.

Psalm 77:14 HCSB

Today's Prayer of Grace

Lord, You have promised never to leave me or forsake me. You are always with me, protecting me and encouraging me. Whatever this day may bring, I thank You for Your love and for Your strength. Let me lean upon You, Father, this day and forever. Amen

Day 69

THE LIGHT OF THE WORLD

I have come as a light into the world, so that everyone who believes in Me would not remain in darkness.

John 12:46 HCSB

The Bible says that you are "the light that gives light to the world." The Bible also says that you should live in a way that lets other people understand what it means to be a follower of Jesus.

What kind of light have you been giving off? Hopefully, you've been a good example for everybody to see. Why? Because the world needs all the light it can get, and that includes your light, too!

The old familiar hymn begins, "What a friend we have in Jesus . . . ." No truer words were ever penned. Jesus is the sovereign Friend and ultimate Savior of mankind. Christ showed enduring love for you by willingly sacrificing His own life so that you might have eternal life. As a response to His sacrifice, you should love Him, praise Him, and share His message of salvation with your neighbors and with the world.

Do you seek to be an extreme follower of Christ? Then you must let your light shine . . . today and every day.

If we guard some corner of darkness in ourselves, we will soon be drawing someone else into darkness, shutting them out from the light in the face of Jesus Christ.

Elisabeth Elliot

If we do not radiate the light of Christ around us, the sense of the darkness that prevails in the world will increase.

Mother Teresa

His life is our light—our purpose and meaning and reason for living.

Anne Graham Lotz

God's guidance is even more important than common sense. I can declare that the deepest darkness is outshone by the light of Jesus.

Corrie ten Boom

Go. This is the command of our Lord. Where? To the world, for it is the world that is on God's heart. Out there are multitudes for whom Christ died. And the minute you and I receive the light of the gospel, we, at that moment, become responsible for spreading that light to those who are still in darkness. Granted, we cannot all go physically, but we can go on our knees.

Kay Arthur

You have to look for the joy.
Look for the light of God that is
hitting your life, and you will find
sparkles you didn't know
were there.

—

Barbara Johnson

You are the light that gives light to the world . . . . Live so that they will see the good things you do. Live so that they will praise your Father in heaven.

Matthew 5:14,16 ICB

Then Jesus spoke to them again: "I am the light of the world. Anyone who follows Me will never walk in the darkness, but will have the light of life."

John 8:12 HCSB

TODAY'S PRAYER OF GRACE

Heavenly Father, I praise You for Your Son Jesus, the light of the world and my personal Savior. Let me share His Good News with all who cross my path, and let me share His love with all who need His healing touch. Amen

The Power of Prayer

Don't worry about anything, but in everything,
through prayer and petition with thanksgiving,
let your requests be made known to God.

Philippians 4:6 HCSB

"The power of prayer": these words are so familiar, yet sometimes we forget what they mean. Prayer is a powerful tool for communicating with our Creator; it is an opportunity to commune with the Giver of all things good. Prayer helps us find strength for today and hope for the future. Prayer is not a thing to be taken lightly or to be used infrequently.

Is prayer an integral part of your daily life, or is it a hit-or-miss habit? Do you "pray without ceasing," or is your prayer life an afterthought?

The quality of your spiritual life will be in direct proportion to the quality of your prayer life. Prayer changes things, and it changes you. Today, instead of worrying about your next decision, ask God to lead the way. Don't limit your prayers to meals or to bedtime. Pray constantly about things great and small. God is listening, and He wants to hear from you now.

When the Holy Spirit comes to dwell within us, I believe we gain a built-in inclination to take our concerns and needs to the Lord in prayer.

Shirley Dobson

The center of power is not to be found in summit meetings or in peace conferences. It is not in Peking or Washington or the United Nations, but rather where a child of God prays in the power of the Spirit for God's will to be done in her life, in her home, and in the world around her.

Ruth Bell Graham

We must leave it to God to answer our prayers in His own wisest way. Sometimes, we are so impatient and think that God does not answer. God always answers! He never fails! Be still. Abide in Him.

Mrs. Charles E. Cowman

What God gives in answer to our prayers will always be the thing we most urgently need, and it will always be sufficient.

Elisabeth Elliot

Your family and friends need your prayers and you need theirs. And God wants to hear those prayers. So what are you waiting for?

Marie T. Freeman

God says we don't need to be
anxious about anything;
we just need to pray about
everything.

—

Stormie Omartian

The intense prayer of the righteous is very powerful.

James 5:16 HCSB

Rejoice in hope; be patient in affliction; be persistent in prayer.

Romans 12:12 HCSB

Let the words of my mouth and the meditation of my heart be acceptable in Your sight, O Lord, my strength and my Redeemer.

Psalm 19:14 NKJV

Yet He often withdrew to deserted places and prayed.

Luke 5:16 HCSB

TODAY'S PRAYER OF GRACE

Dear Lord, make me a woman of constant prayer. Your Holy Word commands me to pray without ceasing. In all things great and small, at all times, whether happy or sad, let me seek Your wisdom and Your strength . . . in prayer. Amen

HE FORGIVES US

Your beliefs about these things should be kept secret between you and God. People are happy if they can do what they think is right without feeling guilty.

Romans 14:22 NCV

All of us have sinned. Sometimes our sins result from our own stubborn rebellion against God's commandments. And sometimes, we are swept up in events that are beyond our abilities to control. Under either set of circumstances, we may experience intense feelings of guilt. But God has an answer for the guilt that we feel. That answer, of course, is His forgiveness. When we confess our wrongdoings and repent from them, we are forgiven by the One who created us.

Are you troubled by feelings of guilt or regret? If so, you must repent from your misdeeds, and you must ask your Heavenly Father for His forgiveness. When you do so, He will forgive you completely and without reservation. Then, you must forgive yourself just as God has forgiven you: thoroughly and unconditionally.

If God has forgiven you, why can't you forgive yourself?

Marie T. Freeman

If choosing to spend time alone with God is a real struggle—a heavy-handed demand that only adds more guilt and stress to your already overblown schedule—it's time to change the way you approach his presence.

Doris Greig

Even in long-term grief there is a way to bring closure and to rise above the rage, the guilt, the pain. In Christ this is possible.

Barbara Johnson

Stop blaming yourself and feeling guilty, unworthy, and unloved. Instead begin to say, "If God is for me, who can be against me? God loves me, and I love myself. Praise the Lord, I am free in Jesus' name, amen!"

Joyce Meyer

When I prayerfully remember my shortcomings, I'm not informing the Lord of anything he doesn't already know. But when I enumerate my failings, I take responsibility before him, and he then releases me from dirty shame, grimy guilt, and scummy sin.

Patsy Clairmont

One of Satan's most effective ploys
is to make us believe that
we are small, insignificant,
and worthless.

—

Susan Lenzkes

Be diligent to present yourself approved to God, a worker who doesn't need to be ashamed, correctly teaching the word of truth.

2 Timothy 2:15 HCSB

There is therefore now no condemnation to those who are in Christ Jesus, who do not walk according to the flesh, but according to the Spirit.

Romans 8:1 NKJV

But God, who is abundant in mercy, because of His great love that He had for us, made us alive with the Messiah even though we were dead in trespasses. By grace you are saved!

Ephesians 2:4-5 HCSB

All the prophets testify about Him that through His name everyone who believes in Him will receive forgiveness of sins.

Acts 10:43 HCSB

TODAY'S PRAYER OF GRACE

Dear Lord, thank You for the guilt that I feel when I disobey You. Help me confess my wrongdoings, help me accept Your forgiveness, and help me renew my passion to serve You. Amen

Day 72

The Power of Purpose

The lines of purpose in your lives never grow slack,
tightly tied as they are to your future in heaven,
kept taut by hope.

Colossians 1:5 MSG

"What on earth does God intend for me to do with my life?" It's an easy question to ask but, for many of us, a difficult question to answer. Why? Because God's purposes aren't always clear to us. Sometimes we wander aimlessly in a wilderness of our own making. And sometimes, we struggle mightily against God in an unsuccessful attempt to find success and happiness through our own means, not His.

Sometimes, God's intentions will be clear to you; other times, God's plan will seem uncertain at best. But even on those difficult days when you are unsure which way to turn, you must never lose sight of these overriding facts: God created you for a reason; He has important work for you to do; and He's waiting patiently for you to do it.

And the next step is up to you.

Only God's chosen task for you will ultimately satisfy. Do not wait until it is too late to realize the privilege of serving Him in His chosen position for you.

Beth Moore

In the very place where God has put us, whatever its limitations, whatever kind of work it may be, we may indeed serve the Lord Christ.

Elisabeth Elliot

How much of our lives are, well, so daily. How often our hours are filled with the mundane, seemingly unimportant things that have to be done, whether at home or work. These very "daily" tasks could become a celebration of praise. "It is through consecration," someone has said, "that drudgery is made divine."

Gigi Graham Tchividjian

How do I love God? By doing beautifully the work I have been given to do, by doing simply that which God entrusted to me, in whatever form it may take.

Mother Teresa

His life is our light—our purpose and meaning and reason for living.

Anne Graham Lotz

For it is God who is working among you both the willing and the working for His good purpose.

Philippians 2:13 HCSB

We know that all things work together for the good of those who love God: those who are called according to His purpose.

Romans 8:28 HCSB

I will instruct you and show you the way to go; with My eye on you, I will give counsel.

Psalm 32:8 HCSB

You reveal the path of life to me; in Your presence is abundant joy; in Your right hand are eternal pleasures.

Psalm 16:11 HCSB

TODAY'S PRAYER OF GRACE

Dear Lord, You are the Creator of the universe, and I know that Your plan for my life is grander than I can imagine. Let Your purposes be my purposes, and let me trust in the assurance of Your promises. Amen

TIME FOR RENEWAL

Take My yoke upon you and learn from Me, because I am gentle and humble in heart, and you will find rest for your souls. For My yoke is easy and My burden is light.
Matthew 11:29-30 HCSB

For busy women living in a fast-paced 21st-century world, life may seem like a merry-go-round that never stops turning. If that description seems to fit your life, then you may find yourself running short of patience or strength, or both. If you're feeling tired or discouraged, there is a source from which you can draw the power needed to recharge your spiritual batteries. That source is God.

Are you exhausted or troubled? Turn your heart toward God in prayer. Are you weak or worried? Take the time—or, more accurately, make the time—to delve deeply into God's Holy Word. Are you spiritually depleted? Call upon fellow believers to support you, and call upon Christ to renew your spirit and your life. When you do, you'll discover that the Creator of the universe stands always ready and always able to create a new sense of wonderment and joy in you.

When we reach the end of our strength, wisdom, and personal resources, we enter into the beginning of his glorious provisions.

Patsy Clairmont

Each of us has something broken in our lives: a broken promise, a broken dream, a broken marriage, a broken heart . . . and we must decide how we're going to deal with our brokenness. We can wallow in self-pity or regret, accomplishing nothing and having no fun or joy in our circumstances; or we can determine with our will to take a few risks, get out of our comfort zone, and see what God will do to bring unexpected delight in our time of need.

Luci Swindoll

He is the God of wholeness and restoration.

Stormie Omartian

Repentance removes old sins and wrong attitudes, and it opens the way for the Holy Spirit to restore our spiritual health.

Shirley Dobson

God gives us permission to forget our past and the understanding to live our present. He said He will remember our sins no more. (Psalm 103:11-12)

Serita Ann Jakes

But may the God of all grace, who called us to His eternal glory by Christ Jesus, after you have suffered a while, perfect, establish, strengthen, and settle you.

1 Peter 5:10 NKJV

Finally, brothers, rejoice. Be restored, be encouraged, be of the same mind, be at peace, and the God of love and peace will be with you.

2 Corinthians 13:11 HCSB

But those who wait on the Lord shall renew their strength; they shall mount up with wings like eagles, they shall run and not be weary, they shall walk and not faint.

Isaiah 40:31 NKJV

Therefore if anyone is in Christ, he is a new creature; the old things passed away; behold, new things have come.

2 Corinthians 5:17 HCSB

TODAY'S PRAYER OF GRACE

Lord, You are my rock and my strength. When I grow weary, let me turn my thoughts and my prayers to You. When I am discouraged, restore my faith in You. Let me always trust in Your promises, Lord, and let me draw strength from those promises and from Your unending love. Amen

THE POWER OF OBEDIENCE

*Follow the whole instruction the Lord your God
has commanded you, so that you may live, prosper,
and have a long life in the land you will possess.*

Deuteronomy 5:33 HCSB

How can we demonstrate our love for God? By accepting His Son as our personal Savior and by placing Christ squarely at the center of our lives and our hearts. Jesus said that if we are to love Him, we must obey His commandments (John 14:15). Thus, our obedience to the Master is an expression of our love for Him.

In Ephesians 2:10 we read, "For we are His workmanship, created in Christ Jesus for good works" (NKJV). These words are instructive: We are not saved by good works, but for good works. Good works are not the root, but rather the fruit of our salvation.

Today, let the fruits of your stewardship be a clear demonstration of your love for Christ. When you do, your good heart will bring forth many good things for yourself and for God. Christ has given you spiritual abundance and

271

eternal life. You, in turn, owe Him good treasure from a single obedient heart . . . yours.

Lord, as in heaven Your will is punctually performed, so may it be done on earth by all creatures, particularly in me and by me.

St. Elizabeth of Hungary

I know the power obedience has for making things easy which seem impossible.

St. Teresa of Avila

The pathway of obedience can sometimes be difficult, but it always leads to a strengthening of our inner woman.

Vonette Bright

Rejoicing is a matter of obedience to God—an obedience that will start you on the road to peace and contentment.

Kay Arthur

God is not hard to please. He does not expect us to be absolutely perfect. He just expects us to keep moving toward Him and believing in Him, letting Him work with us to bring us into conformity to His will and ways.

Joyce Meyer

I have sought You with all my heart; don't let me wander from Your commands.

Psalm 119:10 HCSB

Therefore, everyone who hears these words of Mine and acts on them will be like a sensible man who built his house on the rock. The rain fell, the rivers rose, and the winds blew and pounded that house. Yet it didn't collapse, because its foundation was on the rock.

Matthew 7:24–25 HCSB

Just then someone came up and asked Him, "Teacher, what good must I do to have eternal life?" "Why do you ask Me about what is good?" He said to him. "There is only One who is good. If you want to enter into life, keep the commandments."

Matthew 19:16-17 HCSB

TODAY'S PRAYER OF GRACE

Dear Lord, when I obey Your commandments, and when I trust the promises of Your Son, I experience love, peace, and abundance. Direct my path far from the temptations and distractions of this world. And, let me discover Your will and follow it, Dear Lord, this day and always. Amen

THE POWER OF OPTIMISM

Make me to hear joy and gladness.
Psalm 51:8 KJV

Are you an optimistic, hopeful, enthusiastic Christian? You should be. After all, as a believer, you have every reason to be optimistic about life here on earth and life eternal. As C. H. Spurgeon observed, "Our hope in Christ for the future is the mainstream of our joy." But sometimes, you may find yourself pulled down by the inevitable demands and worries of life-here-on-earth. If you find yourself discouraged, exhausted, or both, then it's time to take your concerns to God. When you do, He will lift your spirits and renew your strength.

Today, make this promise to yourself and keep it: vow to be a hope-filled Christian. Think optimistically about your life, your profession, your family, and your future. Trust your hopes, not your fears. Take time to celebrate God's glorious creation. And then, when you've filled your heart with hope and gladness, share your optimism with others. They'll be better for it, and so will you.

We may run, walk, stumble, drive, or fly, but let us never lose sight of the reason for the journey, or miss a chance to see a rainbow on the way.

Gloria Gaither

Make the least of all that goes and the most of all that comes. Don't regret what is past. Cherish what you have. Look forward to all that is to come. And most important of all, rely moment by moment on Jesus Christ.

Gigi Graham Tchividjian

If you can't tell whether your glass is half-empty or half-full, you don't need another glass; what you need is better eyesight . . . and a more thankful heart.

Marie T. Freeman

Developing a positive attitude means working continually to find what is uplifting and encouraging.

Barbara Johnson

The Christian lifestyle is not one of legalistic do's and don'ts, but one that is positive, attractive, and joyful.

Vonette Bright

It never hurts your eyesight to look on the bright side of things.

Barbara Johnson

Yesterday is just experience
but tomorrow is glistening
with purpose—and today
is the channel leading
from one to the other.

—

Barbara Johnson

The Lord is my light and my salvation; whom shall I fear? The Lord is the strength of my life; of whom shall I be afraid?

Psalm 27:1 KJV

For God has not given us a spirit of fearfulness, but one of power, love, and sound judgment.

2 Timothy 1:7 HCSB

I can do everything through him that gives me strength.

Philippians 4:13 NIV

Be of good courage, and he shall strengthen your heart, all ye that hope in the LORD.

Psalm 31:24 KJV

TODAY'S PRAYER OF GRACE

Thank You, Lord, for Your infinite love. Make me an optimistic Christian, Father, as I place my hope and my trust in You. Amen

Your Passion for Life

Never be lacking in zeal,
but keep your spiritual fervor, serving the Lord.
Romans 12:11 NIV

Are you passionate about your life, your loved ones, your work, and your Savior? As a believer who has been saved by a risen Christ, you should be.

Why did Christ endure the humiliation and torture of the cross? He did it for you. His love is as near as your next breath, as personal as your next thought, more essential than your next heartbeat. And what must you do in response to the Savior's gifts? You must accept His love, praise His name, and share His message of salvation. And, you must conduct yourself in a manner that demonstrates to all the world that your acquaintance with the Master is not a passing fancy, but that it is, instead, the cornerstone and the touchstone of your life.

Our world desperately needs faithful believers who are passionate about their lives and their faith. Be such a believer. The world desperately needs your enthusiasm, and just as importantly, you need the experience of sharing it.

When you allow Christ to reign over your heart—when you worship Him with words, thoughts, prayers, and deeds—your life can become a glorious adventure. When you live passionately—and share your passion with others—God will most certainly bless you and yours . . . today and forever.

Exploring the desire of our hearts
is not a waste of time.
It is precisely the place
where God is stirring.

—

Paula Rinehart

Give me the love that leads the way, the faith that nothing can dismay, the hope no disappointments tire, the passion that will burn like fire. Let me not sink to be a clod: Make me thy fuel, flame of God.

Amy Carmichael

Life is too short to spend it being angry, bored, or dull.

Barbara Johnson

Gratitude unlocks the fullness of life. It turns what we have into enough, and more. It turns denial into acceptance, chaos to order, confusion to clarity. It can turn a meal into a feast, a house into a home, a stranger into a friend. Gratitude makes sense of our past, brings peace for today, and creates a vision for tomorrow.

Melody Beattie

The most characteristic mark of a great mind is to choose some one important object and pursue it for life.

Anna Letitia Barbauld

Finding your passion is the single most important ingredient for changing your world.

Nicole Johnson

He did it with all his heart. So he prospered.

2 Chronicles 31:21 NKJV

In all the work you are doing, work the best you can. Work as if you were doing it for the Lord, not for people.

Colossians 3:23 NCV

I have seen that there is nothing better than for a person to enjoy his activities, because that is his reward. For who can enable him to see what will happen after he dies?

Ecclesiastes 3:22 HCSB

Souls who follow their hearts thrive; fools bent on evil despise matters of soul.

Proverbs 13:19 MSG

Today's Prayer of Grace

Dear Lord, thank You for the gift of Your Son Jesus, my personal Savior. Let me be a worthy disciple of Christ, and let me be ever grateful for His love. I offer my life to You, Lord, so that I might live with passion and with purpose. I will praise You always as I give thanks for Your Son and for Your everlasting love. Amen

Pleasing God

The person who knows my commandments and keeps them,
that's who loves me. And the person who loves me
will be loved by my Father, and I will love him
and make myself plain to him.

John 14:21 MSG

When God made you, He equipped you with an array of talents and abilities that are uniquely yours. It's up to you to discover those talents and to use them, but sometimes the world will encourage you to do otherwise. At times, society will attempt to cubbyhole you, to standardize you, and to make you fit into a particular, preformed mold. Perhaps God has other plans.

Sometimes, because you're an imperfect human being, you may become so wrapped up in meeting society's expectations that you fail to focus on God's expectations. To do so is a mistake of major proportions—don't make it. Instead, seek God's guidance as you focus your energies on becoming the best "you" that you can possibly be. And, when it comes to matters of conscience, seek approval not from your peers, but from your Creator.

Whom will you try to please today: God or man? Your primary obligation is not to please imperfect men and women. Your obligation is to strive diligently to meet the expectations of an all-knowing and perfect God. Trust Him always. Love Him always. Praise Him always. And seek to please Him. Always.

Get ready for God to show you
not only His pleasure, but His approval.

—

Joni Eareckson Tada

Make God's will the focus of your life day by day. If you seek to please Him and Him alone, you'll find yourself satisfied with life.

Kay Arthur

If you are receiving your affirmation, love, self worth, joy, strength and acceptance from anywhere but God, He will shake it.

Lisa Bevere

You will get untold flak for prioritizing God's revealed and present will for your life over man's . . . but, boy, is it worth it.

Beth Moore

If you really want to please God and intend to be in full agreement with His will, you can't go wrong.

Francis Mary Paul Libermann

God is not hard to please. He does not expect us to be absolutely perfect. He just expects us to keep moving toward Him and believing in Him, letting Him work with us to bring us into conformity to His will and ways.

Joyce Meyer

Obviously, I'm not trying to be a people pleaser! No, I am trying to please God. If I were still trying to please people, I would not be Christ's servant.

Galatians 1:10 NLT

Be energetic in your life of salvation, reverent and sensitive before God. That energy is God's energy, an energy deep within you, God himself willing and working at what will give him the most pleasure.

Philippians 2:12-13 MSG

Everything that goes into a life of pleasing God has been miraculously given to us by getting to know, personally and intimately, the One who invited us to God. The best invitation we ever received!

2 Peter 1:3 MSG

TODAY'S PRAYER OF GRACE

Dear Lord, today I will honor You with my thoughts, my actions, and my prayers. I will seek to please You, and I will strive to serve You. Your blessings are as limitless as Your love. And because I have been so richly blessed, I will worship You, Father, with thanksgiving in my heart and praise on my lips, this day and forever. Amen

SHARING THE GOOD NEWS

I will also make You a light of the nations so that
My salvation may reach to the end of the earth.

Isaiah 49:6 NASB

After His resurrection, Jesus addressed His disciples:

But the eleven disciples proceeded to Galilee, to the mountain which Jesus had designated. When they saw Him, they worshiped Him; but some were doubtful. And Jesus came up and spoke to them, saying, "All authority has been given to Me in heaven and on earth. Go therefore and make disciples of all the nations, baptizing them in the name of the Father and the Son and the Holy Spirit, teaching them to observe all that I commanded you; and lo, I am with you always, even to the end of the age" (Matthew 28:16–20 NASB).

Christ's great commission applies to Christians of every generation, including our own. Jesus commanded His disciples to become fishers of men. We must do likewise, and we must do so today. Tomorrow may indeed be too late.

Those who are not yet in the family of Christ need us to be his hands, his feet, his eyes, his ears, and his voice to help them find God's love.

Doris Greig

Being an extrovert isn't essential to evangelism—obedience and love are.

Rebecca Manley Pippert

We are now, a very, very few feeble workers, scattering the grain broadcast according as time and strength permit. God will give the harvest; doubt it not. But the laborers are few.

Lottie Moon

It never ceases to amaze me the way the Lord creates a bond among believers which reaches across continents, beyond race and color.

Corrie ten Boom

Our commission is quite specific. We are told to be His witness to all nations. For us, as His disciples, to refuse any part of this commission frustrates the love of Jesus Christ, the Son of God.

Catherine Marshall

But you will receive power when the Holy Spirit has come upon you, and you will be My witnesses in Jerusalem, in all Judea and Samaria, and to the ends of the earth.

Acts 1:8 HCSB

After this the Lord appointed 70 others, and He sent them ahead of Him in pairs to every town and place where He Himself was about to go. He told them: "The harvest is abundant, but the workers are few. Therefore, pray to the Lord of the harvest to send out workers into His harvest. Now go; I'm sending you out like lambs among wolves."

Luke 10:1-3 HCSB

Then He said to them, "Go into all the world and preach the gospel to the whole creation."

Mark 16:15 HCSB

TODAY'S PRAYER OF GRACE

Heavenly Father, every man and woman, every boy and girl is Your child. You desire that all Your children know Jesus as their Lord and Savior. Father, let me be part of Your Great Commission. Let me give, let me pray, and let me go out into this world so that I might be a fisher of men . . . for You. Amen

DAY 79

REAL REPENTANCE

Come back to the LORD and live!
Amos 5:6 NLT

Who among us has sinned? All of us. But, God calls upon us to turn away from sin by following His commandments. And the good news is this: When we do ask God's forgiveness and turn our hearts to Him, He forgives us absolutely and completely.

Genuine repentance requires more than simply offering God apologies for our misdeeds. Real repentance may start with feelings of sorrow and remorse, but it ends only when we turn away from the sin that has heretofore distanced us from our Creator. In truth, we offer our most meaningful apologies to God, not with our words, but with our actions. As long as we are still engaged in sin, we may be "repenting," but we have not fully "repented."

Is there an aspect of your life that is distancing you from your God? If so, ask for His forgiveness, and—just as importantly—stop sinning. Then, wrap yourself in the protection of God's Word. When you do, you will be secure.

There is nothing that God cannot forgive except for the rejection of Christ. No matter how black the sin, how hideous the sin, if we but confess it to Him in true repentance and faith, He will forgive. He will accept and forgive.

Ruth Bell Graham

In repentance, we must be truly sorry for our sin, and we must express our intent to turn away from it.

Shirley Dobson

When true repentance comes, God will not hesitate for a moment to forgive, cast the sins in the sea of forgetfulness, and put the child on the road to restoration.

Beth Moore

Real repentance is always accompanied by godly sorrow. Asking God to forgive us for a sin we are not yet sorry we committed is a waste of time.

Beth Moore

When I prayerfully remember my shortcomings, I'm not informing the Lord of anything he doesn't already know. But when I enumerate my failings, I take responsibility before him, and he then releases me from dirty shame, grimy guilt, and scummy sin.

Patsy Clairmont

Four marks of true repentance are: acknowledgement of wrong, willingness to confess it, willingness to abandon it, and willingness to make restitution.

—

Corrie ten Boom

If we say, "We have no sin," we are deceiving ourselves, and the truth is not in us. If we confess our sins, He is faithful and righteous to forgive us our sins and to cleanse us from all unrighteousness.

1 John 1:8-9 HCSB

There will be more joy in heaven over one sinner who repents than over 99 righteous people who don't need repentance.

Luke 15:7 HCSB

But the Pharisees and their scribes were complaining to His disciples, "Why do you eat and drink with tax collectors and sinners?" Jesus replied to them, "The healthy don't need a doctor, but the sick do. I have not come to call the righteous, but sinners to repentance."

Luke 5:30-32 HCSB

Today's Prayer of Grace

When I stray from Your commandments, Lord, I must not only confess my sins, I must also turn from them. When I fall short, help me to change. When I reject Your Word and Your will for my life, guide me back to Your side. Forgive my sins, Dear Lord, and help me live according to Your plan for my life. Your plan is perfect, Father; I am not. Let me trust in You. Amen

DAY 80

HIS PERSPECTIVE . . . AND YOURS

Since you have been raised to new life with Christ,
set your sights on the realities of heaven, where Christ sits at
God's right hand in the place of honor and power.

Colossians 3:1 NLT

For most of us, life is busy and complicated. Amid the rush and crush of the daily grind, it is easy to lose perspective . . . easy, but wrong. When our world seems to be spinning out of control, we can regain perspective by slowing ourselves down and then turning our thoughts and prayers toward God.

Do you carve out quiet moments each day to offer thanksgiving and praise to your Creator? You should. During these moments of stillness, you will often sense the love and wisdom of our Lord.

The familiar words of Psalm 46:10 remind us to "Be still, and know that I am God" (NKJV). When we do so, we encounter the awesome presence of our loving Heavenly Father, and we are blessed beyond words. But, when we ignore the presence of our Creator, we rob ourselves of His perspective, His peace, and His joy.

Today and every day, make time to be still before God. When you do, you can face the day's complications with the wisdom and power that only He can provide.

Attitude is the mind's paintbrush;
it can color any situation.

—

Barbara Johnson

Instead of being frustrated and overwhelmed by all that is going on in our world, go to the Lord and ask Him to give you His eternal perspective.

Kay Arthur

When we look at the individual parts of our lives, some things appear unfair and unpleasant. When we take them out of the context of the big picture, we easily drift into the attitude that we deserve better, and the tumble down into the pit of pride begins.

Susan Hunt

Like a shadow declining swiftly . . . away . . . like the dew of the morning gone with the heat of the day; like the wind in the treetops, like a wave of the sea, so are our lives on earth when seen in light of eternity.

Ruth Bell Graham

Gratitude unlocks the fullness of life. It turns what we have into enough, and more. It turns denial into acceptance, chaos to order, confusion to clarity. It can turn a meal into a feast, a house into a home, a stranger into a friend. Gratitude makes sense of our past, brings peace for today, and creates a vision for tomorrow.

Melody Beattie

All I'm doing right now, friends, is showing how these things pertain to Apollos and me so that you will learn restraint and not rush into making judgments without knowing all the facts. It is important to look at things from God's point of view. I would rather not see you inflating or deflating reputations based on mere hearsay.

1 Corinthians 4:6 MSG

But Martha was pulled away by all she had to do in the kitchen. Later, she stepped in, interrupting them. "Master, don't you care that my sister has abandoned the kitchen to me? Tell her to lend me a hand." The Master said, "Martha, dear Martha, you're fussing far too much and getting yourself worked up over nothing. One thing only is essential, and Mary has chosen it— it's the main course, and won't be taken from her."

Luke 10:40-42 MSG

TODAY'S PRAYER OF GRACE

Dear Lord, give me wisdom and perspective. Guide me according to Your plans for my life and according to Your commandments. And keep me mindful, Dear Lord, that Your truth is—and will forever be—the ultimate truth. Amen

YOUR POTENTIAL

Have faith in the Lord your God, and you will stand strong.
Have faith in his prophets, and you will succeed.

2 Chronicles 20:20 NCV

D o you expect your future to be bright? Are you willing to dream king-sized dreams . . . and are you willing to work diligently to make those dreams happen? Hopefully so—after all, God promises that we can do "all things" through Him. Yet most of us live far below our potential. We take half measures; we dream small dreams; we waste precious time and energy on the distractions of the world. But God has other plans for us.

In her diary, Anne Frank wrote, "The good news is that you really don't know how great you can be, how much you can love, what you can accomplish, and what your potential is." These words apply to you. You possess great potential, potential that you must use or forfeit. And the time to fulfill that potential is now.

Freedom from the rule of sin releases the potential for which we were created—to reflect the glory of the Glorious One.

Susan Hunt

Kids are great. They are exciting. Their potential is simply phenomenal. And in any given family there is the potential to change the world for God.

Maxine Hancock

Don't bypass the potential for meaningful friendships just because of differences. Explore them. Embrace them. Love them.

Luci Swindoll

God created us with an overwhelming desire to soar. He designed us to be tremendously productive and "to mount up with wings like eagles," realistically dreaming of what He can do with our potential.

Carol Kent

I am more and more persuaded that all that is required of us is faithful seed-sowing. The harvest is bound to follow.

Annie Armstrong

Let us not become weary in doing good, for at the proper time we will reap a harvest if we do not give up.

Galatians 6:9 NIV

His lord said unto him, Well done, thou good and faithful servant: thou hast been faithful over a few things, I will make thee ruler over many things: enter thou into the joy of thy lord.

Matthew 25:21 KJV

Commit your activities to the Lord and your plans will be achieved.

Proverbs 16:3 HCSB

TODAY'S PRAYER OF GRACE

Lord, You have blessed me with a love that is far beyond my limited understanding. You loved me before I was ever born; You sent Your Son Jesus to redeem me from my sins; You have given me the gift of eternal life. And, You have given me special talents; let me use those talents to the best of my ability and to the glory of Your kingdom so that I might be a good and faithful servant this day and forever. Amen

DAY 82

YOUR REASONS TO REJOICE

Set your minds on what is above,
not on what is on the earth.
Colossians 3:2 HCSB

The Christian life is a cause for celebration, but sometimes we don't feel much like celebrating. In fact, when the weight of the world seems to bear down upon our shoulders, celebration may be the last thing on our minds . . . but it shouldn't be. As God's children, we are all blessed beyond measure on good days and bad. This day is a non-renewable resource—once it's gone, it's gone forever. We should give thanks for this day while using it for the glory of God.

What will be your attitude today? Will you be fearful, angry, bored, or worried? Will you be cynical, bitter, or pessimistic? If so, God wants to have a little talk with you.

God created you in His own image, and He wants you to experience joy and abundance. But, God will not force His joy upon you; you must claim it for yourself. So today, and every day hereafter, celebrate the life that God has given you. Think optimistically about yourself and your future. Give thanks to the One who has given you everything, and trust in your heart that He wants to give you so much more.

Optimism is that faith that leads to achievement.
Nothing can be done without hope and confidence.

—

Helen Keller

Each one of us is responsible for our own happiness. If we choose to allow ourselves to become miserable and unhappy, the problem is ours, not someone else's.

Joyce Meyer

I could go through this day oblivious to the miracles all around me, or I could tune in and "enjoy."

Gloria Gaither

The things we think are the things that feed our souls. If we think on pure and lovely things, we shall grow pure and lovely like them; and the converse is equally true.

Hannah Whitall Smith

Some people complain that God put thorns on roses, while others praise Him for putting roses on thorns.

Anonymous

If we could change our attitudes, we should not only see life differently, but life itself would come to be different. Life would undergo a change of appearance because we ourselves had undergone a change of attitude.

Katherine Mansfield

A miserable heart means a miserable life; a cheerful heart fills the day with a song.

Proverbs 15:15 MSG

For the word of God is living and active. Sharper than any double-edged sword, it penetrates even to dividing soul and spirit, joints and marrow; it judges the thoughts and attitudes of the heart.

Hebrews 4:12 NIV

Your attitude should be the same as that of Christ Jesus: Who, being in very nature God, did not consider equality with God something to be grasped, but made himself nothing, taking the very nature of a servant, being made in human likeness. And being found in appearance as a man, he humbled himself and became obedient to death—even death on a cross!

Philippians 2:5-8 NIV

TODAY'S PRAYER OF GRACE

Lord, I have so many reasons to be thankful; let my attitude be a reflection of the many blessings I have received. Make me a woman whose thoughts are Christlike and whose hopes are worthy of the One who has given me so much. Amen

DAY 83

Today's Theme: Honesty

THE BEST POLICY

Therefore, putting away lying, "Let each one of you speak truth with his neighbor," for we are members of one another.

Ephesians 4:25 NKJV

It has been said on many occasions and in many ways that honesty is the best policy. For believers, it is far more important to note that honesty is God's policy. And if we are to be servants worthy of our Savior, Jesus Christ, we must be honest and forthright in our communications with others.

Sometimes, honesty is difficult; sometimes, honesty is painful; always, honesty is God's commandment. In the Book of Exodus, God did not command, "Thou shalt not bear false witness when it is convenient." And He didn't say, "Thou shalt not bear false witness most of the time." God said, "Thou shalt not bear false witness against thy neighbor." Period.

Sometime soon, perhaps even today, you will be tempted to bend the truth or perhaps even to break it. Resist that temptation. Truth is God's way . . . and it must also be yours. Period.

Those who are given to white lies soon become color blind.

Anonymous

A person who really cares about his or her neighbor, a person who genuinely loves others, is a person who bears witness to the truth.

Anne Graham Lotz

We must learn, then, to relate transparently and genuinely to others because that is God's style of relating to us.

Rebecca Manley Pippert

Much guilt arises in the life of the believer from practicing the chameleon life of environmental adaptation.

Beth Moore

The single most important element in any human relationship is honesty—with oneself, with God, and with others.

Catherine Marshall

One thing that is important for stable emotional health is honesty—with self and with others.

Joyce Meyer

And what about this piece of trivia: "If you shake hands on a promise, that's nothing; but if you raise your hand that God is your witness, that's serious"? What ridiculous hairsplitting! What difference does it make whether you shake hands or raise hands? A promise is a promise. What difference does it make if you make your promise inside or outside a house of worship? A promise is a promise. God is present, watching and holding you to account regardless.

Matthew 23:18-20 MSG

But when he, the Spirit of truth, comes, he will guide you into all truth . . . .

John 16:13 NIV

Jesus answered, "I am the way and the truth and the life. No one comes to the Father except through me."

John 14:6 NIV

TODAY'S PRAYER OF GRACE

Lord, You are a God of truth; let me be a woman of truth. Sometimes speaking the truth is difficult, but when I am weak or fearful, Lord, give me the strength to speak words that are worthy of the One who created me, so that others might see Your eternal truth reflected in my words and my deeds. Amen

Day 84

THE POISON OF ENVY

Let us not become boastful, challenging one another,
envying one another.
Galatians 5:26 NASB

Because we are frail, imperfect human beings, we are sometimes envious of others. But God's Word warns us that envy is sin. Thus, we must guard ourselves against the natural tendency to feel resentment and jealousy when other people experience good fortune.

As believers, we have absolutely no reason to be envious of any people on earth. After all, as Christians we are already recipients of the greatest gift in all creation: God's grace. We have been promised the gift of eternal life through God's only begotten Son, and we must count that gift as our most precious possession.

Rather than succumbing to the sin of envy, we should focus on the marvelous things that God has done for us— starting with Christ's sacrifice. And we must refrain from preoccupying ourselves with the blessings that God has chosen to give others.

So here's a surefire formula for a happier, healthier life: Count your own blessings and let your neighbors count theirs. It's the godly way to live.

Never indulge in jealousy or envy.
Those two destructive emotions
will eat you alive.

—

Loretta Young

What God asks, does, or requires of others is not my business; it is His.

Kay Arthur

The hard part about being a praying wife is maintaining a pure heart. If you have resentment, anger, unforgiveness, or an ungodly attitude—even if there's good reason for it—you'll have a difficult time seeing answers to your prayers. But if you can release those feelings to God in total honesty, there is nothing that can change a marriage more dramatically.

Stormie Omartian

Instead of allowing the pain in our lives to shape our character, taking us through rivers of humility and brokenness, we can let the sorrow become overwhelming, choking out life, filling us instead with bitterness and resentment.

Angela Thomas

Discontent dries up the soul.

Elisabeth Elliot

An envious heart makes a treacherous ear.

Zora Neale Hurston

So rid yourselves of all wickedness, all deceit, hypocrisy, envy, and all slander.

1 Peter 2:1 HCSB

Do not covet your neighbor's house . . . or anything that belongs to your neighbor.

Exodus 20:17 HCSB

If your sinful nature controls your mind, there is death. But if the Holy Spirit controls your mind, there is life and peace.

Romans 8:6 NLT

For where envy and selfish ambition exist, there is disorder and every kind of evil.

James 3:16 HCSB

TODAY'S PRAYER OF GRACE

Dear Lord, You are the Giver of all good gifts. Today I will praise You for my blessings, and I won't be envious of the blessings You've given to others. Amen

DAY 85

HIS TRUTH

You will know the truth, and the truth will set you free.
John 8:32 HCSB

God is vitally concerned with truth. His Word teaches the truth; His Spirit reveals the truth; His Son leads us to the truth. When we open our hearts to God, and when we allow His Son to rule over our thoughts and our lives, God reveals Himself, and we come to understand the truth about ourselves and the Truth (with a capital T) about God's gift of grace.

The familiar words of John 8:32 remind us that when we come to know God's Truth, we are liberated. Have you been liberated by that Truth? And are you living in accordance with the eternal truths that you find in God's Holy Word? Hopefully so.

Today, as you fulfill the responsibilities that God has placed before you, ask yourself this question: "Do my thoughts and actions bear witness to the ultimate Truth that God has placed in my heart, or am I allowing the pressures of everyday life to overwhelm me?" It's a profound question that deserves an answer . . . now.

The difficult truth about truth is that it often requires us to change our perspectives, attitudes, and rules for living.

Susan Lenzkes

To worship Him in truth means to worship Him honestly, without hypocrisy, standing open and transparent before Him.

Anne Graham Lotz

Those who walk in truth walk in liberty.

Beth Moore

The Holy Spirit was given to guide us into all truth, but He doesn't do it all at once.

Elisabeth Elliot

Having truth decay? Brush up on your Bible!

Anonymous

"You are a king then?" Pilate asked. "You say that I'm a king," Jesus replied. "I was born for this, and I have come into the world for this: to testify to the truth. Everyone who is of the truth listens to My voice."

John 18:37 HCSB

For God's wrath is revealed from heaven against all godlessness and unrighteousness of people who by their unrighteousness suppress the truth.

Romans 1:18 HCSB

These are the things you must do: Speak truth to one another; render honest and peaceful judgments in your gates.

Zechariah 8:16 HCSB

Be diligent to present yourself approved to God, a worker who doesn't need to be ashamed, correctly teaching the word of truth.

2 Timothy 2:15 HCSB

Today's Prayer of Grace

Heavenly Father, You are the way and the truth and the light. Today—as I follow Your way and share Your Good News—let me be a worthy example to others and a worthy servant to You. Amen

Day 86

Setting the Right Example

You are the light that gives light to the world. . . .
In the same way, you should be a light for other people.
Live so that they will see the good things you do
and will praise your Father in heaven.

Matthew 5:14,16 NCV

Whether we like it or not, all of us are role models. Our friends and family members watch our actions and, as followers of Christ, we are obliged to act accordingly.

What kind of example are you? Are you the kind of woman whose life serves as a genuine example of righteousness? Are you a woman whose behavior serves as a positive role model for young people? Are you the kind of woman whose actions, day in and day out, are based upon kindness, faithfulness, and a love for the Lord? If so, you are not only blessed by God, but you are also a powerful force for good in a world that desperately needs positive influences such as yours.

Don't worry about what
you do not understand.
Worry about what you
do understand in the Bible
but do not live by.

—

Corrie ten Boom

In your desire to share the gospel, you may be the only Jesus someone else will ever meet. Be real and be involved with people.

Barbara Johnson

The religion of Jesus Christ has an ethical as well as a doctrinal side.

Lottie Moon

In serving we uncover the greatest fulfillment within and become a stellar example of a woman who knows and loves Jesus.

Vonette Bright

Our trustworthiness implies His trustworthiness.

Beth Moore

There is nothing anybody else can do that can stop God from using us. We can turn everything into a testimony.

Corrie ten Boom

As we live moment by moment under the control of the Spirit, His character, which is the character of Jesus, becomes evident to those around us.

Anne Graham Lotz

You should be an example to the believers in speech, in conduct, in love, in faith, in purity.

1 Timothy 4:12 HCSB

Do everything without grumbling and arguing, so that you may be blameless and pure.

Philippians 2:14–15 HCSB

Set an example of good works yourself, with integrity and dignity in your teaching.

Titus 2:7 HCSB

For the kingdom of God is not in talk but in power.

1 Corinthians 4:20 HCSB

TODAY'S PRAYER OF GRACE

Lord, make me a worthy example to my family and friends. And, let my words and my deeds serve as a testimony to the changes You have made in my life. I will praise You, Father, by following in the footsteps of Your Son so that others may see Him through me. Amen

Focusing on God, Not Fear

But He said to them, "Why are you fearful,
O you of little faith?" Then He arose and rebuked the winds
and the sea, and there was a great calm.

Matthew 8:26 NKJV

A frightening storm rose quickly on the Sea of Galilee, and the disciples were afraid. Because of their limited faith, they feared for their lives. When they turned to Jesus, He calmed the waters and He rebuked His disciples for their lack of faith in Him.

On occasion, we, like the disciples, are frightened by the inevitable storms of life. Why are we afraid? Because we, like the disciples, possess imperfect faith.

When we genuinely accept God's promises as absolute truth, when we trust Him with life-here-on-earth and life eternal, we have little to fear. Faith in God is the antidote to worry. Faith in God is the foundation of courage and the source of power. Today, let us trust God more completely and, by doing so, move beyond our fears to a place of abundance, assurance, and peace.

God did away with all my fear. It was time for someone to stand up—or in my case, sit down. So I refused to move.

Rosa Parks

God knows that the strength that comes from wrestling with our fear will give us wings to fly.

Paula Rinehart

His hand on me is a father's hand, gently guiding and encouraging. His hand lets me know he is with me, so I am not afraid.

Mary Morrison Suggs

Fear knocked at the door. Faith answered. No one was there.

Anonymous

Let nothing disturb you, nothing frighten you; all things are passing; God never changes.

St. Teresa of Avila

Facing our deepest fears means making peace with our seen self and with our unseen self.

Sheila Walsh

Even when I go through the darkest valley, I fear [no] danger, for You are with me.

Psalm 23:4 HCSB

Don't be afraid. Only believe.

Mark 5:36 HCSB

For I, the Lord your God, hold your right hand and say to you: Do not fear, I will help you.

Isaiah 41:13 HCSB

I sought the Lord, and He heard me, and delivered me from all my fears.

Psalm 34:4 NKJV

TODAY'S PRAYER OF GRACE

Father, even when I walk through the valley of the shadow of death, I will fear no evil because You are with me. Thank You, Lord, for Your perfect love, a love that casts out fear and gives me strength and courage to meet the challenges of this world. Amen

Day 88

Keep Growing!

When I was a child, I spoke and thought and reasoned
as a child does. But when I grew up,
I put away childish things.

1 Corinthians 13:11 NLT

If you are to grow as a woman, you need both knowledge and wisdom. Knowledge is found in textbooks. Wisdom, on the other hand, is found through experience, through years of trial and error, and through careful attention to the Word of God. Knowledge is an important building block in a well-lived life, and it pays rich dividends both personally and professionally. But, wisdom is even more important because it refashions not only your mind, but also your heart.

When it comes to your faith, God doesn't intend for you to stand still. He wants you to keep growing as a woman and as a spiritual being. No matter how "grown-up" you may be, you still have growing to do. And the more you grow, the more lovely you become, inside and out.

You are either becoming more like Christ every day or you're becoming less like Him. There is no neutral position in the Lord.

Stormie Omartian

He does not need to transplant us into a different field. He transforms the very things that were before our greatest hindrances, into the chief and most blessed means of our growth. No difficulties in your case can baffle Him. Put yourself absolutely into His hands, and let Him have His own way with you.

Elisabeth Elliot

Growth in depth and strength and consistency and fruitfulness and ultimately in Christlikeness is only possible when the winds of life are contrary to personal comfort.

Anne Graham Lotz

The whole idea of belonging to Christ is to look less and less like we used to and more and more like Him.

Angela Thomas

Wisdom enlarges our capacity for discovery and delight, causing wonder to grow as we grow.

Susan Lenzkes

You cannot grow spiritually until
you have the assurance
that Christ is in your life.

—

Vonette Bright

Therefore, laying aside all malice, all deceit, hypocrisy, envy, and all evil speaking, as newborn babes, desire the pure milk of the word, that you may grow thereby.

1 Peter 2:1-2 NKJV

Consider it a great joy, my brothers, whenever you experience various trials, knowing that the testing of your faith produces endurance. But endurance must do its complete work, so that you may be mature and complete, lacking nothing.

James 1:2-4 HCSB

This is why I remind you to keep using the gift God gave you when I laid my hands on you. Now let it grow, as a small flame grows into a fire.

2 Timothy 1:6 NCV

Today's Prayer of Grace

Dear Lord, when I open my heart to You, I am blessed. Today, I will praise You, Father, as I accept Your love and Your wisdom. And, I will do my best to continue to grow in my faith every day that I live. Amen

Today's Theme: Celebration

CELEBRATING HIS GIFTS

Is anyone happy? Let him sing songs of praise.
James 5:13 NIV

The 100th Psalm reminds us that the entire earth should "Shout for joy to the Lord." As God's children, we are blessed beyond measure, but sometimes, as busy women living in a demanding world, we are slow to count our gifts and even slower to give thanks to the Giver.

Our blessings include life and health, family and friends, freedom and possessions—for starters. And, the gifts we receive from God are multiplied when we share them. May we always give thanks to God for His blessings, and may we always demonstrate our gratitude by sharing our gifts with others.

The 118th Psalm reminds us that, "This is the day which the LORD has made; let us rejoice and be glad in it" (v. 24, NASB). May we celebrate this day and the One who created it.

When the dream of our heart is one that God has planted there, a strange happiness flows into us. At that moment, all of the spiritual resources of the universe are released to help us. Our praying is then at one with the will of God and becomes a channel for the Creator's purposes for us and our world.

Catherine Marshall

Joy is a by-product not of happy circumstances, education or talent, but of a healthy relationship with God and a determination to love Him no matter what.

Barbara Johnson

God knows everything. He can manage everything, and He loves us. Surely this is enough for a fullness of joy that is beyond words.

Hannah Whitall Smith

According to Jesus, it is God's will that His children be filled with the joy of life.

Catherine Marshall

If you can forgive the person you were, accept the person you are, and believe in the person you will become, you are headed for joy. So celebrate your life.

Barbara Johnson

Christ is the secret, the source,
the substance, the center,
and the circumference of all true
and lasting gladness.

—

Mrs. Charles E. Cowman

This is the day the LORD has made; we will rejoice and be glad in it.

Psalm 118:24 NKJV

Rejoice in the Lord always. I will say it again: Rejoice!

Philippians 4:4 HCSB

David and the whole house of Israel were celebrating before the Lord.

2 Samuel 6:5 HCSB

Their sorrow was turned into rejoicing and their mourning into a holiday. They were to be days of feasting, rejoicing, and of sending gifts to one another and the poor.

Esther 9:22 HCSB

TODAY'S PRAYER OF GRACE

Lord God, You have created a grand and glorious universe that is far beyond human understanding. The heavens proclaim Your handiwork, and every star in the sky tells of Your power. Let me celebrate You and Your marvelous creation, Father, and let me give thanks for this day. Today is Your gift to me, Lord. Let me use it to Your glory while giving all the praise to You. Amen

He Blesses
the Righteous

The LORD approves of those who are good,
but he condemns those who plan wickedness.

Proverbs 12:2 NLT

If you want to know God, you should obey God. But obeying Him isn't always easy. You live in a world that presents countless temptations to stray far from God's path. So here's some timely advice: when you're confronted with sin, walk—or better yet run—in the opposite direction.

When you seek righteousness for yourself—and when we seek the companionship of people who do likewise—you will reap the spiritual rewards that God has in store for you. When you live in accordance with God's commandments, you will be blessed. When you genuinely seek to follow in the footsteps of God's Son, you will experience God's presence, God's peace, and God's abundance.

So make yourself this promise: Support only those activities that further God's kingdom and your own spiritual growth. Then, prepare to reap the blessings that God has promised to all those who live according to His will and His Word.

Holiness is not God's asking us to be "good";
it is an invitation to be "His."

—

Lisa Bevere

Holiness has never been the driving force of the majority. It is, however, mandatory for anyone who wants to enter the kingdom.

Elisabeth Elliot

He doesn't need an abundance of words. He doesn't need a dissertation about your life. He just wants your attention. He wants your heart.

Kathy Troccoli

We are in desperate need for women of faith who are willing to courageously stand against sin and stand for righteousness.

Susan Hunt

Our afflictions are designed not to break us but to bend us toward the eternal and the holy.

Barbara Johnson

Becoming pure is a process of spiritual growth, and taking seriously the confession of sin during prayer time moves that process along, causing us to purge our life of practices that displease God.

Elizabeth George

Because the eyes of the Lord are on the righteous and His ears are open to their request. But the face of the Lord is against those who do evil.

1 Peter 3:12 HCSB

Therefore, come out from among them and be separate, says the Lord; do not touch any unclean thing, and I will welcome you.

2 Corinthians 6:17 HCSB

And now, Israel, what does the Lord your God ask of you except to fear the Lord your God by walking in all His ways, to love Him, and to worship the Lord your God with all your heart and all your soul?

Deuteronomy 10:12 HCSB

Today's Prayer of Grace

Holy, Holy, Holy . . . You are a righteous and holy God, and You have called me to be Your righteous servant. When I fall short, forgive me, Father, and renew a spirit of holiness within me. Lead me, Lord, along Your path, and guide me far from the temptations of this world. Let Your Holy Word guide my actions, and let Your love reside in my heart, this day and every day. Amen

Day 91

ENCOURAGING WORDS FOR FAMILY AND FRIENDS

So encourage each other and give each other strength,
just as you are doing now.
1 Thessalonians 5:11 NCV

Are you a woman who is a continuing source of encouragement to your family and friends? Hopefully so. After all, one of the reasons that God put you here is to serve and encourage other people—starting with the people who live under your roof.

In his letter to the Ephesians, Paul writes, "Do not let any unwholesome talk come out of your mouths, but only what is helpful for building others up according to their needs, that it may benefit those who listen" (v. 29 NIV). This passage reminds us that, as Christians, we are instructed to choose our words carefully so as to build others up through wholesome, honest encouragement. How can we build others up? By celebrating their victories and their accomplishments. As the old saying goes, "When someone does something good, applaud—you'll make two people happy."

Today, look for the good in others and celebrate the good that you find. When you do, you'll be a powerful force of encouragement in your corner of the world . . . and a worthy servant to your God.

Encouragement is to a friendship
what confetti is to a party.

—

Nicole Johnson

If someone listens or stretches out a hand or whispers a word of encouragement or attempts to understand a lonely person, extraordinary things begin to happen.

Loretta Girzartis

True friends will always lift you higher and challenge you to walk in a manner pleasing to our Lord.

Lisa Bevere

Words. Do you fully understand their power? Can any of us really grasp the mighty force behind the things we say? Do we stop and think before we speak, considering the potency of the words we utter?

Joni Eareckson Tada

The overall goal in helping any individual is to communicate hope, that they might more courageously and confidently face daily life with its trials and struggles.

Verna Birkey

Don't forget that a single sentence, spoken at the right moment, can change somebody's whole perspective on life. A little encouragement can go a long, long way.

Marie T. Freeman

I want their hearts to be encouraged and joined together in love, so that they may have all the riches of assured understanding, and have the knowledge of God's mystery—Christ.

Colossians 2:2 HCSB

Carry one another's burdens; in this way you will fulfill the law of Christ.

Galatians 6:2 HCSB

But encourage each other daily, while it is still called today, so that none of you is hardened by sin's deception.

Hebrews 3:13 HCSB

And let us be concerned about one another in order to promote love and good works.

Hebrews 10:24 HCSB

TODAY'S PRAYER OF GRACE

Dear Lord, because I am Your child, I am blessed. You have loved me eternally, cared for me faithfully, and saved me through the gift of Your Son Jesus. Just as You have lifted me up, Lord, let me also lift up others in a spirit of encouragement and hope. And, if I can help even a single person, Lord, may the glory be Yours. Amen

DAY 92

Today's Theme: Fellowship

THE POWER OF FELLOWSHIP

*Don't you realize that all of you together are the temple
of God and that the Spirit of God lives in you?*
1 Corinthians 3:16 NLT

You can guard your steps by associating yourself with a faithful group of fellow believers—and that's precisely what you should do. Your association with fellow Christians should be uplifting, enlightening, encouraging, and consistent. In short, fellowship with other believers should be an integral part of your everyday life.

When you make a habit of spending time with likeminded believers, you'll enhance your own life, and theirs. Plus, you'll be protecting yourself (and them) against the inevitable temptations and distractions that have become so commonplace in our modern society. So what are you waiting for? The answer, of course, is that you shouldn't wait another minute . . . you should reach out to your brothers and sisters in Christ, starting right now. And you should keep reaching out as long as you live.

Are you an active member of your own fellowship? Are you a builder of bridges inside the four walls of your church and outside it? Do you contribute to God's glory by contributing your time and your talents to a close-knit band of believers? Hopefully so. The fellowship of believers is intended to be a powerful tool for spreading God's Good News and uplifting His children. God intends for you to be a fully contributing member of that fellowship. Your intentions should be the same.

―――――――――――

Christians are like coals of a fire.
Together they glow—apart they grow cold.

—

Anonymous

In God's economy you will be hard-pressed to find many examples of successful "Lone Rangers."

Luci Swindoll

It is wonderful to have all kinds of human support systems, but we must always stand firm in God and in Him alone.

Joyce Meyer

One of the ways God refills us after failure is through the blessing of Christian fellowship. Just experiencing the joy of simple activities shared with other children of God can have a healing effect on us.

Anne Graham Lotz

Be united with other Christians. A wall with loose bricks is not good. The bricks must be cemented together.

Corrie ten Boom

Only when we realize that we are indeed broken, that we are not independent, that we cannot do it ourselves, can we turn to God and take that which he has given us, no matter what it is, and create with it.

Madeleine L'Engle

How good and pleasant it is when brothers can live together!

Psalm 133:1 HCSB

Now I urge you, brothers, in the name of our Lord Jesus Christ, that you all say the same thing, that there be no divisions among you, and that you be united with the same understanding and the same conviction.

1 Corinthians 1:10 HCSB

The one who loves his brother remains in the light, and there is no cause for stumbling in him.

1 John 2:10 HCSB

Now finally, all of you should be like-minded and sympathetic, should love believers, and be compassionate and humble.

1 Peter 3:8 HCSB

TODAY'S PRAYER OF GRACE

Heavenly Father, You have given me a community of supporters called the church, and I praise You for that gift. Let our church's fellowship be a reflection of the love we feel for each other and the love we feel for You. Amen

FOLLOWING CHRIST

But whoever keeps His word, truly in him the love of God is perfected. This is how we know we are in Him: the one who says he remains in Him should walk just as He walked.

1 John 2:5-6 HCSB

Jesus walks with you. Are you walking with Him? Hopefully, you will choose to walk with Him today and every day of your life.

Jesus loved you so much that He endured unspeakable humiliation and suffering for you. How will you respond to Christ's sacrifice? Will you take up His cross and follow Him (Luke 9:23), or will you choose another path? When you place your hopes squarely at the foot of the cross, when you place Jesus squarely at the center of your life, you will be blessed. If you seek to be a worthy disciple of Jesus, you must acknowledge that He never comes "next." He is always first.

Do you hope to fulfill God's purpose for your life? Do you seek a life of abundance and peace? Do you intend to be Christian, not just in name, but in deed? Then follow Christ. Follow Him by picking up His cross today and every day that you live. When you do, you will quickly discover that Christ's love has the power to change everything, including you.

As we live moment by moment under the control of the Spirit, His character, which is the character of Jesus, becomes evident to those around us.

—

Anne Graham Lotz

Will you, with a glad and eager surrender, hand yourself and all that concerns you over into his hands? If you will do this, your soul will begin to know something of the joy of union with Christ.

Hannah Whitall Smith

The Christian faith is meant to be lived moment by moment. It isn't some broad, general outline—it's a long walk with a real Person. Details count: passing thoughts, small sacrifices, a few encouraging words, little acts of kindness, brief victories over nagging sins.

Joni Eareckson Tada

You cannot cooperate with Jesus in becoming what He wants you to become and simultaneously be what the world desires to make you. If you would say, "Take the world but give me Jesus," then you must deny yourself and take up your cross. The simple truth is that your "self" must be put to death in order for you to get to the point where for you to live is Christ. What will it be? The world and you, or Jesus and you? You do have a choice to make.

Kay Arthur

Peter said, "No, Lord!" But he had to learn that one cannot say "No" while saying "Lord" and that one cannot say "Lord" while saying "No."

Corrie ten Boom

Then he told them what they could expect for themselves: "Anyone who intends to come with me has to let me lead."

Luke 9:23 MSG

I've laid down a pattern for you. What I've done, you do.

John 13:15 MSG

No one can serve two masters. Either he will hate the one and love the other, or he will be devoted to the one and despise the other.

Matthew 6:24 NIV

Whoever is not willing to carry the cross and follow me is not worthy of me. Those who try to hold on to their lives will give up true life. Those who give up their lives for me will hold on to true life.

Matthew 10:38-39 NCV

TODAY'S PRAYER OF GRACE

Dear Lord, You sent Your Son so that I might have abundant life and eternal life. I praise You, Father, for my Savior, Christ Jesus. I will follow Him, honor Him, and share His Good News, this day and every day. Amen

DAY 94

FORGIVENESS NOW

Be merciful, just as your Father also is merciful.
Luke 6:36 HCSB

The world holds few if any rewards for those who remain angrily focused upon the past. Still, the act of forgiveness is difficult for all but the most saintly men and women. Are you mired in the quicksand of bitterness or regret? If so, you are not only disobeying God's Word, you are also wasting your time.

Being frail, fallible, imperfect human beings, most of us are quick to anger, quick to blame, slow to forgive, and even slower to forget. Yet as Christians, we are commanded to forgive others, just as we, too, have been forgiven.

If there exists even one person—alive or dead—against whom you hold bitter feelings, it's time to forgive. Or, if you are embittered against yourself for some past mistake or shortcoming, it's finally time to forgive yourself and move on. Hatred, bitterness, and regret are not part of God's plan for your life. Forgiveness is.

Forgiveness is actually the best revenge because it not only sets us free from the person we forgive, but it frees us to move into all that God has in store for us.

Stormie Omartian

God expects us to forgive others as He has forgiven us; we are to follow His example by having a forgiving heart.

Vonette Bright

The more you practice the art of forgiving, the quicker you'll master the art of living.

Marie T. Freeman

Have you thought that your willingness to forgive is really your affirmation of the power of God to do you good?

Paula Rinehart

God gives us permission to forget our past and the understanding to live our present. He said He will remember our sins no more. (Psalm 103:11-12)

Serita Ann Jakes

God has been very gracious to me, for I never dwell upon anything wrong which a person has done to me, as to remember it afterwards. If I do remember it, I always see some other virtue in the person.

St. Teresa of Avila

And whenever you stand praying,
if you have anything against anyone,
forgive him, so that your Father in
heaven may also forgive you
your wrongdoing.

—

Mark 11:25 HCSB

All bitterness, anger and wrath, insult and slander must be removed from you, along with all wickedness. And be kind and compassionate to one another, forgiving one another, just as God also forgave you in Christ.

Ephesians 4:31-32 HCSB

See to it that no one repays evil for evil to anyone, but always pursue what is good for one another and for all.

1 Thessalonians 5:15 HCSB

A person's insight gives him patience, and his virtue is to overlook an offense.

Proverbs 19:11 HCSB

And forgive us our sins, for we ourselves also forgive everyone in debt to us.

Luke 11:4 HCSB

Today's Prayer of Grace

Dear Lord, You have forgiven me; let me show my thankfulness to You by offering forgiveness to others. Today, let forgiveness rule my heart, even when forgiveness is difficult. Let me be Your obedient servant, Lord, and let me be a woman who forgives others just as You have forgiven me. Amen

CHEERFUL GENEROSITY

So let each one give as he purposes in his heart,
not grudgingly or of necessity; for God loves a cheerful giver.
2 Corinthians 9:7 NKJV

The thread of generosity is woven—completely and inextricably—into the very fabric of Christ's teachings. As He sent His disciples out to heal the sick and spread God's message of salvation, Jesus offered this guiding principle: "Freely you have received, freely give" (Matthew 10:8 NIV). The principle still applies. If we are to be disciples of Christ, we must give freely of our time, our possessions, and our love.

Lisa Whelchel spoke for Christian women everywhere when she observed, "The Lord has abundantly blessed me all of my life. I'm not trying to pay Him back for all of His wonderful gifts; I just realize that He gave them to me to give away." All of us have been blessed, and all of us are called to share those blessings without reservation.

Today, make this pledge and keep it: Be a cheerful, generous, courageous giver. The world needs your help, and you need the spiritual rewards that will be yours when you share your possessions, your talents, and your time.

How can we withhold from another what God has so generously allowed us to use and enjoy?

Jan Winebrenner

The Christian gives all she knows of herself to all she knows of God and continues to grow in the knowledge of both.

Gladys Hunt

A cup that is already full cannot have more added to it. In order to receive the further good to which we are entitled, we must give of that which we have.

Margaret Becker

What is your focus today? Joy comes when it is Jesus first, others second . . . then you.

Kay Arthur

Keep in mind that the true measure of an individual is how he treats a person who can do him absolutely no good.

Ann Landers

We can't do everything, but can we do anything more valuable than invest ourselves in another?

Elisabeth Elliot

*The one who has two shirts must
share with someone who has none,
and the one who has food
must do the same.*

—

Luke 3:11 HCSB

Dear friend, you are showing your faith by whatever you do for the brothers, and this you are doing for strangers.

3 John 1:5 HCSB

In every way I've shown you that by laboring like this, it is necessary to help the weak and to keep in mind the words of the Lord Jesus, for He said, "It is more blessed to give than to receive."

Acts 20:35 HCSB

Bear one another's burdens, and so fulfill the law of Christ.

Galatians 6:2 NKJV

If a brother or sister is without clothes and lacks daily food, and one of you says to them, "Go in peace, keep warm, and eat well," but you don't give them what the body needs, what good is it?

James 2:15–16 HCSB

TODAY'S PRAYER OF GRACE

Lord, You have been so generous with me; let me be generous with others. Help me to give generously of my time and my possessions as I care for those in need. And, make me a humble giver, Lord, so that all the glory and the praise might be Yours. Amen

Day 96

PUTTING GOD FIRST

Honor GOD with everything you own; give him the first and the best. Your barns will burst, your wine vats will brim over.

Proverbs 3:9-10 MSG

As you think about the nature of your relationship with God, remember this: you will always have some type of relationship with Him—it is inevitable that your life must be lived in relationship to God. The question is not if you will have a relationship with Him; the burning question is whether that relationship will be one that seeks to honor Him . . . or not.

Are you willing to place God first in your life? And, are you willing to welcome God's Son into your heart? Unless you can honestly answer these questions with a resounding yes, then your relationship with God isn't what it could be or should be. Thankfully, God is always available, He's always ready to forgive, and He's waiting to hear from you now. The rest, of course, is up to you.

I lived with Indians who made pots out of clay which they used for cooking. Nobody was interested in the pot. Everybody was interested in what was inside. The same clay taken out of the same riverbed, always made in the same design, nothing special about it. Well, I'm a clay pot, and let me not forget it. But, the excellency of the power is of God and not us.

Elisabeth Elliot

Make God's will the focus of your life day by day. If you seek to please Him and Him alone, you'll find yourself satisfied with life.

Kay Arthur

Jesus challenges you and me to keep our focus daily on the cross of His will if we want to be His disciples.

Anne Graham Lotz

The greatest honor you can give Almighty God is to live gladly and joyfully because of the knowledge of His love.

Juliana of Norwich

The Holy Spirit testifies of Jesus. So when you are filled with the Holy Spirit, you speak about our Lord and really live to His honor.

Corrie ten Boom

Spiritual worship is focusing
all we are on all He is.

—

Beth Moore

You shall have no other gods before Me.

Exodus 20:3 NKJV

Be careful not to forget the Lord.

Deuteronomy 6:12 HCSB

Jesus answered, "'Love the Lord your God with all your heart, all your soul, and all your mind.' This is the first and most important command."

Matthew 22:37-38 NCV

Those who worship false gods turn their backs on all God's mercies. But I will offer sacrifices to you with songs of praise, and I will fulfill all my vows. For my salvation comes from the LORD alone.

Jonah 2:8-9 NLT

TODAY'S PRAYER OF GRACE

Dear Lord, Your love is eternal and Your laws are everlasting. When I obey Your commandments, I am blessed. Today, I invite You to reign over every corner of my heart. I will have faith in You, Father. I will sense Your presence; I will accept Your love; I will trust Your will; and I will praise You for the Savior of my life: Your Son Jesus. Amen

DAY 97

THE POWER OF
YOUR THOUGHTS

People's thoughts can be like a deep well,
but someone with understanding can find the wisdom there.
Proverbs 20:5 NCV

How will you direct your thoughts today? Will you dwell upon those things that are honorable, true, and worthy of praise (Philippians 4:8)? Or will you allow your thoughts to be hijacked by the negativity that seems to dominate our troubled world?

God intends that you be an ambassador for Him, an enthusiastic, hope-filled Christian. But God won't force you to adopt a positive attitude. It's up to you to think positively about your blessings and opportunities . . . or not. So, today and every day hereafter, celebrate this life that God has given you by focusing your thoughts and your energies upon "things that are excellent and worthy of praise." Today, count your blessings instead of your hardships. And thank the Giver of all things good for gifts that are simply too numerous to count.

The things we think are the things that feed our souls. If we think on pure and lovely things, we shall grow pure and lovely like them; and the converse is equally true.

Hannah Whitall Smith

Attitude is the mind's paintbrush; it can color any situation.

Barbara Johnson

No matter how little we can change about our circumstances, we always have a choice about our attitude toward the situation.

Vonette Bright

As we have by faith said no to sin, so we should by faith say yes to God and set our minds on things above, where Christ is seated in the heavenlies.

Vonette Bright

I am amazed at my own "rut-think" that periodically takes over.

Marilyn Meberg

Preoccupy my thoughts with your praise beginning today.

Joni Eareckson Tada

Come near to God, and God will come near to you. You sinners, clean sin out of your lives. You who are trying to follow God and the world at the same time, make your thinking pure.

James 4:8 NCV

Those who are pure in their thinking are happy, because they will be with God.

Matthew 5:8 NCV

And now, dear brothers and sisters, let me say one more thing as I close this letter. Fix your thoughts on what is true and honorable and right. Think about things that are pure and lovely and admirable. Think about things that are excellent and worthy of praise.

Philippians 4:8 NLT

Today's Prayer of Grace

Dear Lord, keep my thoughts focused on Your love, Your power, Your promises, and Your Son. When I am worried, I will turn to You for comfort; when I am weak, I will turn to You for strength; when I am troubled, I will turn to You for patience and perspective. Help me guard my thoughts, Father, so that I may honor You today and every day that I live. Amen

PRAISING HIM FOR THIS DAY

*Teach us to number our days carefully
so that we may develop wisdom in our hearts.*

Psalm 90:12 HCSB

This day is a gift from God. How will you use it? Will you celebrate God's gifts and obey His commandments? Will you share words of encouragement and hope with all who cross your path? Will you share the Good News of the risen Christ? Will you trust in the Father and praise His glorious handiwork? The answer to these questions will determine, to a surprising extent, the direction and the quality of your day.

The familiar words of Psalm 118:24 remind us of a profound yet simple truth: "This is the day which the LORD hath made; we will rejoice and be glad in it" (KJV). For Christian believers, every day begins and ends with God and His Son. Christ came to this earth to give us abundant life and eternal salvation. We give thanks to our Maker when we treasure each day and use it to the fullest.

Every day of our lives
we make choices about
how we're going to live that day.

—

Luci Swindoll

Each day, each moment is so pregnant with eternity that if we "tune in" to it, we can hardly contain the joy.

Gloria Gaither

Submit each day to God, knowing that He is God over all your tomorrows.

Kay Arthur

Every day we live is a priceless gift of God, loaded with possibilities to learn something new, to gain fresh insights.

Dale Evans Rogers

Today is mine. Tomorrow is none of my business. If I peer anxiously into the fog of the future, I will strain my spiritual eyes so that I will not see clearly what is required of me now.

Elisabeth Elliot

How much of our lives are, well, so daily. How often our hours are filled with the mundane, seemingly unimportant things that have to be done, whether at home or work. These very "daily" tasks could become a celebration of praise. "It is through consecration," someone has said, "that drudgery is made divine."

Gigi Graham Tchividjian

Rejoice in the Lord always. I will say it again: Rejoice!

Philippians 4:4 HCSB

I must work the works of Him who sent Me while it is day; the night is coming when no one can work.

John 9:4 NKJV

Therefore, get your minds ready for action, being self-disciplined, and set your hope completely on the grace to be brought to you at the revelation of Jesus Christ.

1 Peter 1:13 HCSB

TODAY'S PRAYER OF GRACE

Lord, You have given me another day of life; let me celebrate this day, and let me use it according to Your plan. I praise You, Father, for my life and for the friends and family members who make it rich. Enable me to live each moment to the fullest as I give thanks for Your creation, for Your love, and for Your Son. Amen

Trust Him

Trust in the LORD with all your heart; do not depend on
your own understanding. Seek his will in all you do,
and he will direct your paths.

Proverbs 3:5-6 NLT

Open your Bible to its center, and you'll find the Book of Psalms. In it are some of the most beautiful words ever translated into the English language, with none more beautiful than the 23rd Psalm. David describes God as being like a shepherd who cares for His flock. No wonder these verses have provided comfort and hope for generations of believers.

On occasion, you will confront circumstances that trouble you to the very core of your soul. When you are afraid, trust in God. When you are worried, turn your concerns over to Him. When you are anxious, be still and listen for the quiet assurance of God's promises. And then, place your life in His hands. He is your shepherd today and throughout eternity. Trust the Shepherd.

The only safe place is in the center of God's will. It is not only the safest place. It is also the most rewarding and the most satisfying place to be.

Gigi Graham Tchividjian

Obedience is a foundational stepping stone on the path of God's Will.

Elizabeth George

I believe that in every time and place it is within our power to acquiesce in the will of God—and what peace it brings to do so!

Elisabeth Elliot

The center of power is not to be found in summit meetings or in peace conferences. It is not in Peking or Washington or the United Nations, but rather where a child of God prays in the power of the Spirit for God's will to be done in her life, in her home, and in the world around her.

Ruth Bell Graham

In the Garden of Gethsemane, Jesus went through agony of soul in His efforts to resist the temptation to do what He felt like doing rather than what He knew was God's will for Him.

Joyce Meyer

Let us hold fast the confession of our hope without wavering, for He who promised is faithful.

Hebrews 10:23 NKJV

For we walk by faith, not by sight.

2 Corinthians 5:7 NKJV

The one who understands a matter finds success, and the one who trusts in the Lord will be happy.

Proverbs 16:20 HCSB

For the eyes of the Lord range throughout the earth to show Himself strong for those whose hearts are completely His.

2 Chronicles 16:9 HCSB

TODAY'S PRAYER OF GRACE

Lord, when I trust in things of this earth, I will be disappointed. But, when I put my faith in You, I am secure. You are my rock and my shield. Upon Your firm foundation I will build my life. When I am worried, Lord, let me trust in You. You will love me and protect me, and You will share Your boundless grace today, tomorrow, and forever. Amen

Today's Theme: Eternal Life

THE PRICELESS GIFT OF ETERNAL LIFE

For God so loved the world that He gave His only begotten Son, that whoever believes in Him should not perish but have everlasting life.

John 3:16 NKJV

Ours is not a distant God. Ours is a God who understands—far better than we ever could—the essence of what it means to be human. How marvelous it is that God became a man and walked among us. Had He not chosen to do so, we might feel removed from a distant Creator.

God understands our hopes, our fears, and our temptations. He understands what it means to be angry and what it costs to forgive. He knows the heart, the conscience, and the soul of every person who has ever lived, including you. And God has a plan of salvation that is intended for you. Accept it. Accept God's gift through the person of His Son Christ Jesus, and then rest assured: God walked among us so that you might have eternal life; amazing though it may seem, He did it for you.

I can still hardly believe it. I, with shriveled, bent fingers, atrophied muscles, gnarled knees, and no feeling from the shoulders down, will one day have a new body—light, bright and clothed in righteousness—powerful and dazzling.

Joni Eareckson Tada

If you are a believer, your judgment will not determine your eternal destiny. Christ's finished work on Calvary was applied to you the moment you accepted Christ as Savior.

Beth Moore

It is in giving that we receive, it is in pardoning that we are pardoned, it is in dying that we are born to eternal life.

St. Francis

The gift of God is eternal life, spiritual life, abundant life through faith in Jesus Christ, the Living Word of God.

Anne Graham Lotz

God has promised us abundance, peace, and eternal life. These treasures are ours for the asking; all we must do is claim them. One of the great mysteries of life is why on earth do so many of us wait so very long to lay claim to God's gifts?

Marie T. Freeman

Your choice to either receive
or reject the Lord Jesus Christ
will determine where
you spend eternity.

—

Anne Graham Lotz

And this is the testimony: God has given us eternal life, and this life is in His Son. The one who has the Son has life. The one who doesn't have the Son of God does not have life.

1 John 5:11-12 HCSB

Pursue righteousness, godliness, faith, love, endurance, and gentleness. Fight the good fight for the faith; take hold of eternal life, to which you were called and have made a good confession before many witnesses.

1 Timothy 6:11-12 HCSB

Jesus said to her, "I am the resurrection and the life. The one who believes in Me, even if he dies, will live. Everyone who lives and believes in Me will never die—ever. Do you believe this?"

John 11:25-26 HCSB

Today's Prayer of Grace

Lord, I am only here on this earth for a brief while. But, You have offered me the priceless gift of eternal life through Your Son Jesus. I accept Your gift, Lord, with thanksgiving and praise. Let me share the good news of my salvation with those who need Your healing touch. Amen

I have written these things to you
who believe in the name
of the Son of God,
so that you may know
that you have eternal life.

—

1 John 5:13 HCSB

My Notes from this Study

_____

_____

_____

_____

_____

_____

_____

_____

_____

_____

_____

_____

_____

_____

_____

_____

_____

_____

_____

_____

<u>My Notes from this Study</u>

_____

_____

_____

_____

_____

_____

_____

_____

_____

_____

_____

_____

_____

_____

_____

_____

_____

_____

_____

_____

_____

MY NOTES FROM THIS STUDY

My Notes from this Study

_____

_____

_____

_____

_____

_____

_____

_____

_____

_____

_____

_____

_____

_____

_____

_____

_____

_____

_____

_____

_____

My Notes from this Study

<u>My Notes from this Study</u>

_____

_____

_____

_____

_____

_____

_____

_____

_____

_____

_____

_____

_____

_____

_____

_____

_____

_____

_____

_____

MY NOTES FROM THIS STUDY

My Notes from this Study

_____

_____

_____

_____

_____

_____

_____

_____

_____

_____

_____

_____

_____

_____

_____

_____

_____

_____

_____

_____

MY NOTES FROM THIS STUDY

<u>My Notes from this Study</u>

_____

_____

_____

_____

_____

_____

_____

_____

_____

_____

_____

_____

_____

_____

_____

_____

_____

_____

_____

_____

_____

MY NOTES FROM THIS STUDY

_____

_____

_____

_____

_____

_____

_____

_____

_____

_____

_____

_____

_____

_____

_____

_____

_____

_____

_____

_____

My Notes from this Study

_____

_____

_____

_____

_____

_____

_____

_____

_____

_____

_____

_____

_____

_____

_____

_____

_____

_____

_____

_____